PRINTED PATTERN

PRINTED PATTERN

Printing by hand from potato-prints to silkscreens

Rebecca Drury & Yvonne Drury

Photography by Sophie Drury

A & C BLACK • LONDON

First published in Great Britain in 2010
A&C Black Publishers Limited
36 Soho Square
London W1D 3QY
www.acblack.com

ISBN: 978-14081-0625-9

CIP Catalogue records for this book are
available from the British Library and the
U.S. Library of Congress.

Typeset in 9/14pt Interstate Light

Book design by Gabriella Le Grazie
Commissioning editor: Susan James

Printed and bound in China

A&C Black uses paper produced with elemental
chlorine-free pulp, harvested from managed
sustainable forests.

We would like to dedicate this book to all the people who have inspired and helped us over the years.

INTRODUCTION

We love making patterns and designs, developing new motifs and seeing them grow into designs is so exciting. You never know exactly how a design will turn out; you have an idea, which you develop into a pattern, and voila!, a new design is born. You can then use this design to transform everyday items into very special objects.

Printed pattern can be applied to almost any surface, including fabric, paper, card, ceramics, glass or wood. It can be easy and simple to achieve wonderful effects. Specialist equipment is not always necessary as you can print your own patterns inexpensively and effectively on a kitchen table or worktop at home. A vast array of patterns can be produced, from the textured effect of a linoprint to the crisp starkness of a screenprint.

This book contains simple step-by-step instructions for various types of projects and methods – but mainly it is filled with ideas and inspiration. By showing you how simple it can be to achieve impressive results, we hope to inspire you to explore the world of creating and printing your own patterns. Once you begin experimenting with different techniques, you will see that the possibilities are endless; experimentation is essential as it helps you to explore the processes. The

projects that we have illustrated throughout this book are intended as starting points for your own designs; we hope this will help and encourage you to develop your own style.

We can guarantee that you will make mistakes along the way; even the most experienced designers and printers make mistakes - try not to worry when you do. That is the nature of hand printing; things just do not always turn out the way you expect. Mistakes should not be treated as a negative experience, as you can learn and develop your skills through them. Working out what went wrong, and why, helps you gain a deeper understanding of the techniques and processes. Sometimes, you will even enjoy nice surprises when your unintended outcomes result in 'happy mistakes' - unexpected results that turn out to be fabulous.

You do not need any previous experience or knowledge to make a start on these projects. This book is suitable for anyone, from an absolute beginner to the more experienced. It is designed to help you develop and expand your skills and confidence. We believe that there is an element of creativity within everyone, and we hope that this book helps to release some of your potential. So give printed pattern a go!

INSPIRATION

Inspiration is all around us; colours, shapes, motifs, patterns and textures are all present both in nature, and in manmade environments. Recognising these as potential sources of inspiration is simply about taking the time to pause and observe. Most of the time we are so busy getting on with things, rushing from one place to the next, that we just do not seem to notice what is around us. So stop for a second and take another look, whether it be in your garden, on your way to work or whilst you are shopping. Interesting and unusual patterns, motifs, textures and colour combination are to be found almost everywhere! You will be surprised at what you discover once you start looking and may find that you won't be able to stop.

A simple leaf or flower has so many beautiful qualities of line, shape, colour and texture. If your inspiration is taken from nature, your design is more than likely to have an organic feel. On the other hand, if you look towards manmade structures and the urban environment your design may contain graphic lines and have a geometric structure. Sources of inspiration are everywhere. So unleash your creativity, take that second look. Rip up those paint charts and get creative using nature's own colour palette, and the objects and structures that surround you every day.

Designing your own motifs and patterns inspired by your environment means that the patterns you create will be individual to you; they will reflect who you are and enable you to put your personal stamp on items you are making and decorating. If you decide to use existing patterns and motifs, such as the ones included in the back of this book, you will still produce unique results because you will be using the motifs, choosing the colours, and printing and creating patterns by hand. Your arrangement and placement of the motifs, and the colours and textures will have distinctive and special qualities. The outcome will be a one-off, handmade design.

DEVELOPING IDEAS

Collating imagery

To begin creating your own designs, start collecting inspirational imagery. Keep records in the form of sketches, drawings, photographs or found objects. To develop your collections of inspirational images into design ideas, create moodboards and sketchbooks.

COMPOSING MOOD-BOARDS

A moodboard is a collage of images, text, colours and textures. It is made up of visual information that captures the style and essence of your idea/concept. You can include a range of materials, such as printouts, magazine cut-outs, photographs, textures, fabrics and colour pallets/chips. The collected items and materials are then carefully arranged and fixed in place on paper or card to create your moodboard. Moodboards are normally A2 or A3 size.

SKETCHBOOKS

You can use a sketchbook to collate your ideas; make notes, sketch, paste in photographs and images from magazines. It is like your own personal visual diary. Sketchbooks range in size; a small A5 book is easy to carry around in your bag or pocket, whilst an A4 or A3 book is good to keep at home for developing your ideas. There are no rules; use whatever you feel most comfortable with.

COMPOSITION AND LAYOUT

When you start working on your designs, you need to think about the composition and layout you want to create. Your design should flow, without any awkward gaps or spaces, so you must consider the spacing between motifs and patterns. Try not to create layout ideas that are too complicated as often the simplest designs are the most effective. It is just a matter of striking the right balance between detail and simplicity. Once again, this is something that will improve with practice. Look at other designs that you like and try to analyse what it is that makes them successful in terms of composition and layout. There are many different types of layouts, such as stripes, borders, single motifs and multiple all-over patterns.

GETTING STARTED

It is essential to be well prepared before you begin.
Expensive equipment is not required, but you will
need some basic key tools and materials.

PRINTING SURFACE

A specially-designed printing surface is not required; your kitchen or dining-room table, or kitchen worktop will suffice. You can even print on the floor if you do not have a suitable tabletop. However, do bear in mind, if you are going to be printing for sustained periods of time, that it is important you are in a comfortable position. You do not want be leaning over repeatedly or straining as you risk injuring your back!

What you need is a flat, even surface, if you are printing on paper or card a hard surface is fine. However, if you are going to be printing on fabric, particularly using a silk screen, your printing surface should be slightly soft – it should have a little 'give'. The easiest way to achieve this is to pad your surface; a blanket covered with either a cotton sheet or a piece of calico, then stretched over the tabletop, pulled taut, and secured works very well. Using a piece of plywood, chipboard or medium-density fibreboard (MDF) and covering this with the blanket and calico is an even better idea. This you can pull tight, making sure it is wrinkle-free, and then fix it using a staple gun on the underside to secure the padding in place. This way, you will always have a printing surface ready, you can just place it on your table, worktop or floor, and you are ready to go!

BASICS

You will need:

Water. Make sure you have a water supply close by. You will need water to clean your tools and equipment - your kitchen sink, shower or bath are all ideal water supplies.

Scrap paper/newspaper. Keep a plentiful supply of scrap paper as it is very useful to protect your work surface.

Cloths/rags. Paper/kitchen towel. These are great for cleaning up - you can never have too many cloths and rags!

Scissors or a sharp craft knife.

Old spoons and jars. These are useful for mixing and storing your inks and dyes. Start collecting!

Apron/old clothes and gloves. It is always a good idea to wear an apron or old clothes when you are printing - it can be a messy business!

Masking tape.

Hairdryer. A hairdryer is great for drying off your prints and equipment and speeding up the process.

MATERIALS

There is a vast array of materials available to print on: fabric, paper, card, wood, plastic and ceramics are just a few. You can obtain all of these in a variety of surfaces, colours and finishes; the choice is immense. When selecting materials or items do bear in mind that some are easier to print onto than others. Experience will teach you the pros and cons of printing on different materials and surfaces. However, it is good to keep an open mind and test and experiment with a variety of materials, as sometimes the more challenging bases can provide the most interesting results.

Useful tips

● Always ensure you have extra materials so you can carry out test prints and experiment with samples before you start on your final pieces.

● White, natural and lighter-coloured materials are more straightforward to print onto. On these surfaces your print will really stand out. If you have a darker-coloured material that you wish to work with, make sure that your ink/paint is opaque (rather than transparent), otherwise your print may not show up.

● In general, it is easier to print onto flatter surfaces, i.e., those that are not too textured. That said, interesting results can be obtained on textured surfaces - experimentation is the key here!

● When printing onto any products which have a back, such as bags, T-shirts or cushions, you must always place a sheet of thin card inside between the two layers. This will stop any ink seeping through onto the back layer.

INKS

As with the vast choice of possible materials, there is an extensive range of inks and dyes to choose from. You will find a suitable printing ink for each and every type of material you wish to print on.

Different inks have different characteristics, whether they are glossy, matt, opaque or translucent. The main difference between inks is whether they are water-based or oil-based. We mainly use water-based inks to print on fabric; these are easier to clean off equipment and clothes. They are, in general, also more environmentally friendly.

Oil-based inks require specialist solvents for cleaning. Therefore, if using oil-based inks, make sure you work in a well-ventilated area. Oil-based inks are not suitable for processes such as potato printing, as they do not stick to moist surfaces. You must also be careful to dispose of any waste in a responsible manner, and try to limit the amount of ink residue entering the water-system.

COLOURS

Experiment with colour. Finer colours can be achieved by mixing inks together, rather than just using the inks straight from the container. Instead of using a pre-mixed green, for example, try mixing a green using yellow and blue. You can then add a little white to make the colour paler and more pastel. Or add a little black if you want your colour to be more muted.

Useful tips

● Always read the manufacturers' instructions and follow their directions closely.

● Try experimenting with small amounts first, to minimise wastage.

● Strong or dark colours can have a dramatic effect when mixing inks; just a few drops can significantly change the look of the final colour.
When mixing, do not use too many colours as this always produces a muddy outcome.

● When mixing inks, use the same type of ink/dyes. For example, do not mix water-based ink with oil-based ink, or gouache with an acrylic.

● When mixing, keep a record of the colours and amounts you are using as you mix, so that you can replicate the final colour if required.

● Always test your colour on the material you are going to be using, as the base colour can significantly alter the colour of the print.

RELIEF PRINTING

POTATO PRINTING

Potato printing is one of the easiest and most
accessible methods of relief printing; it is also a simple
and inexpensive technique. It represents a naïve,
hand-printed style. However, that's not to say that
it is just for children. If you choose the right pattern
and consider your colours carefully, you can produce
beautiful and tasteful results.

When selecting your motif to make the potato stamp, it is better to choose a design with simple shapes and lines, as these are easy to cut. An elaborate pattern that is overly detailed does not work as well with potato printing, as it is difficult to cut and can look messy.

CUSHION You can use a plain cushion or make your own cushion from scratch. You can be as adventurous as you like when selecting a design for a cushion. Repeating patterns and engineered prints both work well on cushions. Think about tying in colours from your home.

Materials list

Raw potatoes - baking potatoes work best

Paints and inks

Paintbrushes and sponge

Lino-cutting/wood-cutting tool or small knife

Paper towel

Tracing paper

Pencil or pen

Fabric, paper (or whatever you are printing on)

Preparing your potato

First, select your motif.

Cut the potato in half.

Dry out any moisture by placing the potato cut-side down on a paper towel.

Draw your motif onto the cut side of the potato with a pencil or marker. A soft dark pencil works best.

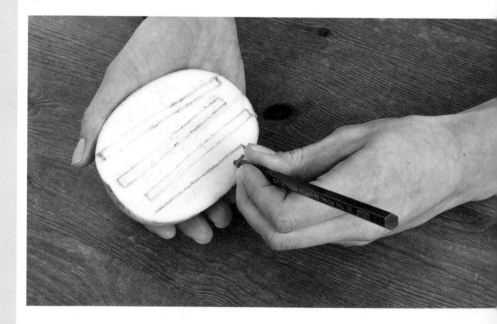

If you are not confident drawing the motif directly onto the potato, begin by drawing the motif onto tracing paper. Lay the tracing paper onto the cut side of the potato. Using a sharp pencil punch a few holes outlining the motif, then remove the tracing paper. You should now be able to draw your design on to the potato by joining up the holes that you made. A bit like dot-to-dot pictures!

Now take your knife or cutting tool and cut around your motif. Make sure your cut is deep enough, around 1cm is fine.

Printing

Apply ink or paint to the potato stamp with a brush or sponge. Remember, the ink should be quite thick. If the ink is too thin it will be very difficult to obtain a successful result.

Before you start, practice by testing your potato stamp on a scrap piece of similar material. This is also the time to experiment with different colour combinations.

Once you are happy with your colours and the results of your test print, you can start to print your design. Remember you need to apply more ink each time you print your motif.

Useful tips

● Try to use an even coating of ink; too much ink will make your print bleed around the edges. Not enough ink will result in a patchy print.

● Remember to apply gentle and even pressure. This can take a little time to perfect, but all it takes is practice.

● Reapply more ink each time you print your motif.

● If you notice that your potato stamp is beginning to lose definition, this could be caused by a build-up of ink. You will need to wipe and gently rinse your stamp, then dry it before continuing.

● Your stamp can be reused for different colours simply by cleaning and drying your potato.

● You can achieve interesting layout options by overprinting your motif. However, you must ensure that each layer is dry before you print on top.

● When printing products which have two layers or a back – e.g., bag, t-shirt or cushion – you must place a sheet of thin card inside between the two layers. This will stop any ink seeping through onto the back layer of your product.

● Your potato stamp should last one or two days. To preserve it for longer, you can wrap it in cling film or seal it in plastic bag and place in your refrigerator (always clean the stamp before storing).

● Never use oil-based inks or paints when printing with potatoes, as oil and water do not mix.

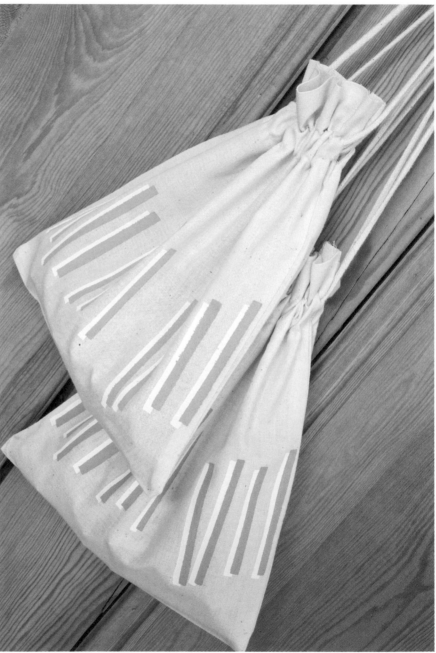

PEG BAGS These simple drawstring bags are useful for a range of things, from pegs to knick-knacks. They would make ideal gift bags.

TABLEMATS Printing your own tablemats is a good way to brighten up mealtimes, or add something special to afternoon tea. They can be used as individual placemats, scattered on the table, or used as a centerpiece.

LINO PRINTING

Linoleum or 'lino' was developed in the 1860s. Lino is made from a mixture of linseed oil, resin and powdered cork with a hessian backing; it is usually grey or light brown in colour. The linocut method of printmaking was first used in Germany in the early 20th century.

Lino printing is a versatile and inexpensive method of printing pattern, it requires only a few tools but offers a wide range of results. Lino blocks can be used for printing onto either fabric or paper. Lino has a flat surface, so the marks you cut into it will have a crisp and distinctive character. It is suitable for broad, bold designs and motifs, which do not contain fine lines. Unlike the potato, lino is quite so durable you so will be able to re-use it many times.

Linocutting chisels or gouges are available in different sizes and have either a V- or U-shaped cutting edge. We suggest that you buy at least one of each shape, as this will enable you to achieve a broader range of marks. Ideally, buy a set that consists of both shapes and a selection of sizes. Lino and linocutting tools are readily available from most art and craft shops.

Make a gift even more special by adding a unique design

Materials list

Lino
Linocutting tools
Paints and inks
Pallet knife or spatula
Small roller
Tracing paper
Pencil or pen
Rolling pin

Making your print

Select your design or motif

Draw your motif onto the lino block with a
pencil or marker. A soft dark pencil works
best.

If you would rather not draw the motif
directly onto the lino, you can draw the
motif onto tracing paper and then transfer
the image onto the lino.

Take your cutting tool and cut around
your motif. Cut away the negative area;
this is the area you do not want to print.
Make sure to always push the chisel or
gouge away from yourself, rather than
pulling it towards you, and try not to cut
too deeply.

Once you are happy with your cut design,
you are ready to apply the ink to the lino.

Mix your ink on a glass/Perspex slab and spread it evenly to make a thin layer. Now take your roller and roll smoothly over the ink, then onto the lino several times in different directions to make sure you achieve an even coat.

Place the lino block face down on the paper or fabric. To print effectively, you must apply even pressure – you can do this with your roller or hand if your block is small. If your block is bigger you can use a rolling pin. Make sure that the block does not move whist you are printing with it; otherwise your results will be blurred and smudged. Then carefully peel back the lino.

You will need to re-apply ink each time you print. You may get a build-up of ink in the cut-away areas, which can cause a loss of definition in your printed design. If this happens wipe away any excess ink with a cloth or paper towel.

Once you have finished printing, wash your lino block and let it air dry thoroughly.

Useful tips

● Always test print first!

● Warm your lino by placing on a radiator or by using a hairdryer -this will make it easier to cut.

● To avoid injury, make sure that you always cut away from your body and keep your non-cutting hand clear of the blade.

● To cut away large areas use the U-shaped tool; to cut more precise details use the V-shaped tool.

● Your linocutting tools will last a long time if you look after them. Do not store them with their blades rubbing against either each other or any other metal objects, as this will damage the cutting edge.

● A paper plate or an old kitchen chopping board can be used for rolling out your inks as an alternative to a piece of acrylic or glass.

Add some sparkle to a pair of trousers

Make a gift even more special by adding a unique design

RUBBER/ERASER PRINTING

Rubber or plastic erasers can be used to make small, striking images. They are great fun, once cut they can be used to print on a variety or surfaces and may be re-used many times. If this method appeals to you, build up a collection that you can dip into to mix and match motifs. A motif created in this way can be used alone or repeated to make an all-over pattern. As erasers are quite small they are ideal for printing smaller items.

Materials list

Plastic or rubber eraser
Paints and inks
Paintbrushes/roller/ink block
Craft knife or lino-/wood-cutting tool
Paper towels
Tracing paper
Pencil
Fabric, paper (or whatever you are printing onto)

Making your print

Start by collecting a selection of plastic or rubber erasers. Try to select a few different shapes and sizes, as this will provide a greater range of options for your designs and motifs. A long, thin eraser is good for stripe designs, while larger, square erasers lend themselves well to bigger motifs.

Select an eraser with at least one flat surface, from which you can cut a motif.

Choose a motif and draw or trace it onto the flat side of the eraser with a pencil.

Use a craft knife or linocutting tools to cut around the edge of the design.

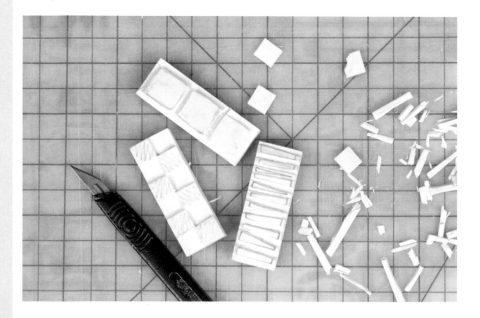

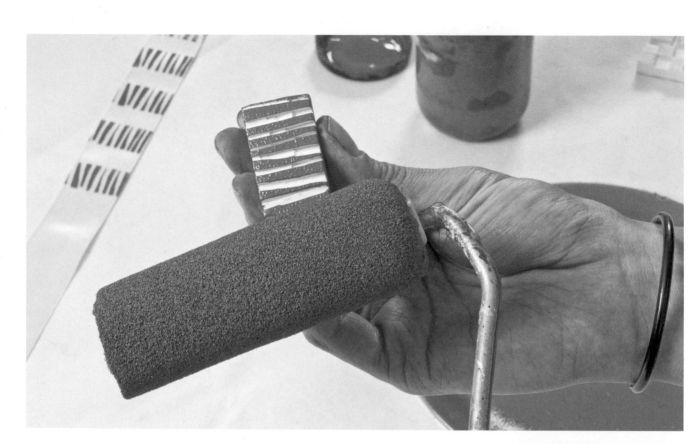

Apply your ink with a brush, roller or inkpad.

To print, simply press the inked surface of the eraser down onto the material you wish to print on. Press firmly but not too hard - remember to practice first on scrap paper or fabric.

Useful tips

● Be careful when cutting out the design, always cut away from your body to avoid accidents.

● Remember that the area that is cut away will be the negative area of your design, i.e., the part that won't print. The areas that remain once the cutting is complete form the motif that will print.

● Rubber erasers are a little easier to cut than plastic ones.

Cheer up your kitchen cupboards with hand-printed paper labels

Hand-printed ribbons add a finishing touch to that special gift

Hand-printed gift tags are another way to personalise gifts for a special occasion.

RUBBER STAMP PRINTING

This has to be one of the easiest and simplest printing methods of all. You can buy rubber stamps from art and craft and stationery shops. They are available in many designs and there is also a good choice of coloured ink pads. Alternatively, you can easily have your own stamp made from your own drawing or design.

Even a laundry bag can be made special by being adventurous.

Materials list

Rubber stamp
Inkpad/sponge roller
Paper or fabric (or whatever you would like to print on)
Ink/paint

Rubber stamps can be printed onto a variety of surfaces. However, achieving a good result on very glossy or textured surfaces may prove more difficult.

Making your print

Ink up your stamp by pressing it onto the inkpad or apply the ink directly to the stamp with a small sponge roller.

Press the stamp firmly onto the printing surface.

That's it!

Useful tips

● Although this is a very simple method, you should still practice first. Different fabrics and materials require different pressure. By practising first you will avoid unnecessary mistakes.

● After repeated printing, the stamp can get a build-up of ink on the backing and edges. If this happens, wipe the edges and backing with a clean cloth or kitchen towel before continuing.

● When you have finished printing with your stamp wash it in warm water, blot it with a cloth and allow it to completely air dry before re-using.

Make a unique statement by customising a skirt.

Handmade cards show that you care

VINTAGE WOODBLOCK PRINTING

Woodcutting is a much more complex and technical process than the others in this section, which requires specific tools and equipment. The actual engraving of the wooden block requires skill, time and patience. Woodblock printing is an ancient process. Wood blocks are known to have existed in northern China since 627 AD. However, they were well established in Europe by the 15th century.

Vintage woodblocks can be found in antique shops, brocantes, flea markets and on e-Bay. They can be brought to life again and re-used; by recycling in this ethical and interesting way you can produce items that are not only unique but also very special.

Materials list

Vintage woodblock
Inks or inkpad/roller
Fabric, paper (or whatever you are
printing onto)

Making your print

Ink up your woodblock by pressing it onto
an inkpad or apply the ink directly to the
woodblock using a small sponge roller. Be
sure to do this evenly and smoothly.

Press the woodblock firmly onto your
printing surface.

Useful tips

● **Refer to rubber stamp printing as both
methods have similar requirements.**

Make a gift extra special by wrapping it in your own woodblock-printed paper.

ROMAN BLINDS Vintage woodblocks can be used on most kinds of fabrics and papers. They are great for decorating plain objects such as these roman blinds.

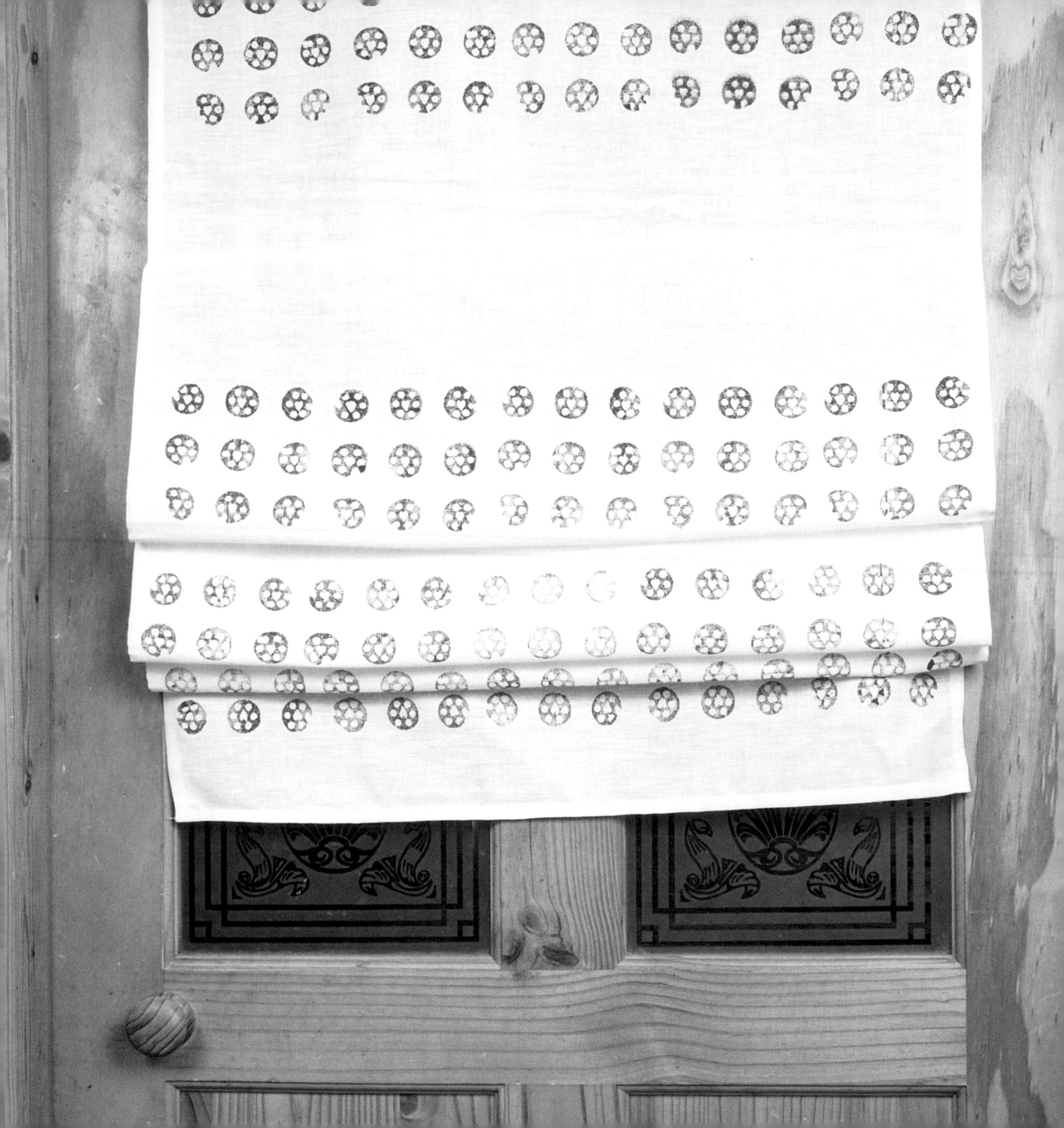

STENCIL PRINTING

Stencilling is a simple and basic print technique. However, it is exceptionally versatile and you can produce some stunning results. It is quite easy to make a stencil and once again it is a process that will not require too many specialist materials or equipment. Stencilling can be used on so many different surfaces - from paper and fabric to walls, floors, furniture and accessories - the possibilities are endless.

Materials list

Thick paper or card, acetate or Mylar
Permanent marker
Scalpel/craft knife
Cutting mat or a piece of thick card
Paints/inks
Masking tape
Stencil brush, sponge or small
sponge roller
Spray mount

You can cut your stencil from many different papers and plastics. The stencil will last longer if it is cut from a plastic-type material, such as acetate or Mylar. It will easily withstand repeated printing and you will be able to wash it and re-use it many times. Acetate is readily available from any stationery store. Mylar is a polyester film commonly used for stencil making and is sold at art supply stores. If you use acetate or Mylar you will be able to spray the backside of your stencil with spray mount. This will make it tacky so it adheres to the material you are printing on and will help stop leakages.

The material you are printing on determines the ink you will need for stencil printing. To apply the ink you can either use a stencil brush, a sponge or a sponge roller. A stencil brush is cylindrical with a flat top, which you use to stipple the ink through the cut stencil. Stencil brushes are available in many different sizes, so can be used for small detail or on larger areas. A sponge can also be used to apply the ink; however, we prefer to use a small sponge-decorating roller. These can be purchased at any DIY or decorating store.

Preparing your stencil

Begin by drawing your design or motif in a sketchbook or on paper.

Once you have finalised your pattern or motif, photocopy your design (at this stage you have the opportunity to change the scale of if you wish).

Lay the photocopy onto a cutting mat and stick down at the corners to secure it. Place the acetate/Mylar on top, sticking this down in place as well to avoid any movement while you are cutting.

Now cut out the design using a sharp scalpel/craft knife; always use a cutting matt or a thick piece of card to protect the surface you are working on.

Printing

Position the cut stencil onto the material you will be printing on, then use either masking tape or spray mount to secure it.

Put the ink on a plate, and load your brush, sponge or roller with ink.

Apply the ink in thin coats to build up a layer. Applying too much ink all at once will result in an uneven print and could cause the design to bleed.

Carefully remove the stencil once the design/motif has been printed. If you plan to use more than one colour or layer, always make sure the ink is dry before staring to print the next layer.

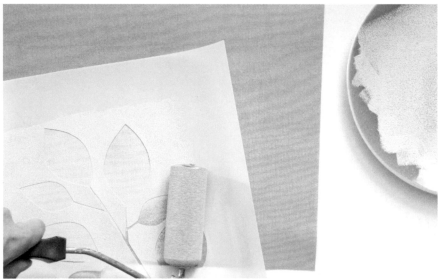

Useful tips

● Ink should not be too runny or 'thin', as it will leak under the stencil and cause your design to bleed.

● Avoid designs with fine, delicate lines, as these will prove too difficult to cut.

● Make sure that the sheet of card/acetate/Mylar is adequately larger than your chosen design/motif – it is important to have plenty of room around your motif as this will help to protect the material you are printing on from splashes and dabs!

● If using more than one colour, it is best to have a different plate, brush or sponge for each ink used.

● Just before you use your acetate or Mylar stencil, spray it underneath with spray mount to make it slightly tacky – this will stop the ink leaking underneath.

● If you are using spray mount, be careful as it is toxic. Avoid inhaling the fumes and wear a protective mask. Always use the spray outside.

● Spray mount may have to be reapplied once it has lost it tackiness.

LAMPSHADE A simple drum lampshade is ideal for stencilling as it has an even surface. Inspiration for this pattern came from the vintage base.

FABRIC WALL HANGING A wall hanging may be slightly more ambitious than you had planned for, but only because of its scale. Don't let this put you off, just give it a go and you will be amazed with the results you can achieve.

CUSHION Why not experiment with different
colour layers. This two-colour stencil creates
a striking contrast on the white cushion.

SHOPPING BAG Do not discard your stencils; they can be re-used many times. Here we have re-used our stencil on a shopping bag; with a change of colour, a whole new look is achieved.

SCREEN PRINTING

There are a variety of different techniques that can be used when printing with silkscreen. Here we are going to cover the three main methods: stencil, screen-filler and photo-emulsion. Screen-printing is great fun and you can achieve some excellent results. The silkscreen enables the ink to be distributed evenly and in a controlled manner.

STENCIL METHOD SCREEN PRINTING

This is a good method for a beginner. It is the simplest and least expensive way to prepare a screen. By cutting a stencil from paper or acetate you can achieve bold and dynamic results. Designs can be cut with scissors, knife or alternatively can be 'torn' to create a textured look. This technique works best with designs and motifs that are bold and do not have too much detail.

Once you have prepared your screen you can work quickly to produce repeat prints one after the other. You can also achieve a high level of detail, especially when using the photo-emulsion method.

Screenprinting is easy to do at home. Screens, inks and equipment can be purchased from any good art and craft supplier. You can print on your kitchen or dining room table and wash off your screen in the kitchen sink or bath.

WALLPAPER/WALL HANGING Hand printed wallpaper can transform any room. By screen-printing a design onto a roll of plain wallpaper you can bring colour and pattern into your surroundings.

STENCIL METHOD

Materials list

Newspaper/newsprint or acetate
Scissors or craft knife
Silkscreen
Squeegee
Inks or paints
Masking tape
Pencil or pen
Fabric, paper (or whatever you are
printing on)

Preparing your screen

First of all, select your design; remember
to choose something without fine detail.

Draw your design onto the newspaper/
newsprint or acetate. You can create a
freehand design or trace an image using
tracing paper.

Now cut out your design or tear the paper
(tearing will create a textured edge to
your design).

You can only use your newspaper/
newsprint stencil a few times, so you will
have to cut more than one. Acetate will
last a lot longer; it can be washed and
re-used many times.

Attach the stencil to the top of the screen
with masking tape.

You are now ready to start test printing.
See printing directions on p. 104.

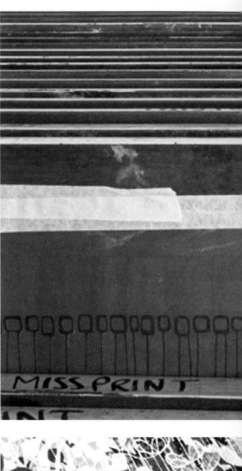

Useful tips

● If using paper, keep it flat and make sure it is not wrinkled.

● Newspaper or newsprint works well for making stencils, but acetate gives better accuracy and durability.

● Your stencils should be slightly smaller than your screen frame.

● Remember to block out any areas in your screen that are not covered by the stencil otherwise the ink will get through and could ruin your print.

● You may be able to use a paper stencil again if it has not moved and is still intact.

TEATOWEL Add a little character to those plain kitchen tea towels. These would also make ideal gifts!

STENCIL FILLER METHOD

Using screen-filler is another simple way of preparing a screen for printing. The screen-filler is painted directly onto the screen to block out those areas you do not wish to print. This allows the ink to be forced through the screen in areas where the screen filler has not been applied. This method allows you to use the same design again and again.

ROLLERBLIND 'Bring the outside in' - by printing a nature inspired print on a roller blind.

SCREEN FILLER METHOD

Material List

Soft pencil
Silkscreen
Screen-filler
Brushes

Preparing your screen

Take a sheet of plain paper and draw your design

Place this layout on a table, then put your screen over this layout and trace your design directly on the screen mesh with a soft lead pencil.

Select an appropriate brush, as this will determine the type of line or texture produced. With a finer brush you will be able to achieve a more detailed design.

Working on the top of the screen, paint the areas of the layout that you do not wish to print. Turn the screen around and brush in any excess screen filler that has seeped through making sure that it is even on both sides. When all areas to be blocked out are covered with screen filler, let the screen dry.

Now hold the screen up to the light to make sure you haven't missed any areas you wanted to cover. If you find any pinholes you will need to spot these in with filler.

Leave to dry thoroughly, preferably overnight.

Your screen is now ready to use, see printing directions on p.104.

Useful tips

● Always read the instructions on the screen filler or emulsion and activator bottles and follow them carefully.

PHOTO-EMULSION METHOD

Using this technique you can achieve a high level
of detail. Your designs can include fine lines,
photographic detail and text. This method may require
more preparation and equipment, but the outcome
possibilities are far greater.

PHOTO -EMULSION METHOD

Material List

Silkscreen
Photo-emulsion kit
Squeegee or piece of card
Artwork (an image of your pattern or
motif, printed in black on a clear acetate)
A clear flat piece of glass or Perspex (no
larger than your screen)
Black paper (larger than your screen)
Light source (a clear incandescent 150
watt bulb)

Preparing your screen

Place your screen on a flat surface with
the top facing up (mesh-side up).

Pour a little the emulsion onto the screen
and, using a squeegee or a piece of card,
spread it as evenly as possible. Don't put
it on too thick. You need as thin and as
even a coat as possible. Any excess can
be scooped back into the pot of emulsion.
You don't have to be a perfectionist – just
do your best.

Once the screen is coated, put it in dark
place to dry. Airing/boiler cupboards
work well.

As soon as your screen is dry, you are
ready to move onto the next step and
expose your image. Do not leave your
screen for too long or the emulsion
will 'bake on' and you will have to start
over again.

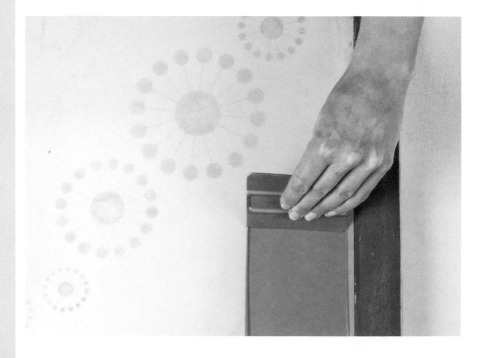

Exposing your screen

Make sure you are prepared with all your materials to hand; once you get the screen out of the dark you need to work swiftly because it will be very sensitive to the light.

Place the screen flat on the piece of black paper with the coated side facing up. The light should be centered above the screen, Do not switch on the light just yet.

Place your artwork on the screen and lay the sheet of glass/Perspex directly over top. Make sure you lay the artwork the correct way. This is especially important if you are using text in your imagery; the text could read backwards if not positioned correctly.

You are now ready to expose your screen. Turn on the light, making sure the light bathes the whole screen.

The exposure time depends on the size of the screen. The following chart is guidance for timings.

SCREEN SIZE	TIME
20 x 25 cm (8"x10")	45 minutes
25 x 36 cm (10"x14")	45 minutes
30 x 46 cm (12"x18")	74 minutes
41 x 51 cm (16"x20")	92 minutes
46 x 51 cm (18"x20")	92 minutes

Once you have exposed your screen, you need to wash it off.

Using a hose, spray your screen with cold water. You will be washing away the emulsion that has been protected by your artwork and so not been hardened by exposure to the light. You can also rub the screen gently to remove any excess emulsion.

You should now see your design being revealed. The design should the same on your screen as on your artwork.

Now dry your screen; you can use a hairdryer to speed up the process.

When your screen is dry, hold it up to the light and check for any areas or pinholes the emulsion has missed. You can fill these using a small brush and some emulsion.

You are now ready to print.

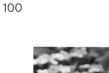

Useful tips

● Follow the instructions on your photo emulsion kit – details will differ between alternative brands and types.

● When drying your screen, a fan heater helps speed up the process.

● Always make sure that your screen artwork is as black as possible, as you do not want the light to penetrate through it. If any light penetrates your design, your screen will be ruined and you will have to start again.

● Exposure times can vary depending on elements such as bulb wattage and the distance of the bulb from the screen. Be prepared to experiment with exposure timings.

● If you do not expose a screen for sufficient time, the image will wash away. If you expose a screen for too long, you will start to lose fine detail of the image.

● You can expose your screen outside in the sun. Even on a cloudy day there are plenty of UV rays you can use to achieve screen exposure.

● If there are areas your emulsion did not wash away from, or in which too much emulsion washed away, you will have to clean your screen and start over again.

PRINTING WITH A SCREEN

Now here is the fun part, printing with your screen.
Whichever screenprinting methods you are using,
the basics for printing with a screen are the same.

TIES Even the dullest items can be brought
to life and jazzed up using screen-printing.

Material List

Silkscreen

Fabric or paper

Masking tape

Squeegee

Inks or paints

Spoon

Rags

Newspaper

Weights to hold down the screen

You will need to prepare an area to print on. Any tabletop is fine. When printing on fabric, your printing surface needs to be slightly soft; it needs to have a little 'give'. So your tabletop/printing area will need padding. A good way to achieve this is to use a blanket with a sheet or a piece of calico over the top. This should be pulled tightly and secured under the table to give a taut, even surface.

As with any new method, screen-printing takes practice; do not worry about making mistakes.

Before you start, practice by testing on a scrap piece of similar material. This is also the time to experiment with different colour combinations and layering.

Once you are happy with your colours and the results of your test print, you can start to print your design.

Lay fabric or paper on the prepared tabletop and secure it with masking tape - this stops any movement whilst printing. Movement can cause blurred results.

Place and position your screen onto the fabric.

Put some weights on the corners of your screen to stop movement when printing. We use bricks wrapped in old tea towels or old weights.

Now place your squeegee at the top end of the screen and spread the ink along below the blade of the squeegee. Holding the squeegee firmly at a 45-degree angle, 'pull' the ink firmly, quickly and smoothly across the screen. You may need more than one 'pull' - so be prepared to repeat this two or three times depending on the ink and the type of fabric you are using.

Carefully lift the screen away from the fabric. Now that you can see the results of your print, you can evaluate whether you need to adjust your printing method. If your print has bled, you may have pressed too hard or used too many pulls. If your print is thin or patchy, this may be due to uneven pressure or not enough pulls.

Once you have finished printing, wash your screen and squeegee as soon as possible to avoid blocking the screen.

Useful tips

● Use gum-strip to tape around the edges of your screen (this will stop the ink seeping through any cracks or gaps between the mesh and the frame). This is the best tape to use, as other sticky tapes can leave a glue residue which is difficult to remove and can damage your screen.

● Try to be experimental. Combine and overprint different motifs together.

● If you are using more than one colour in your design, you will have to use a separate screen, or different area of a large screen, for each different colour/layer.

● Make sure that the ink on your first print is dry before you apply another colour/layer.

● Always start printing with the lightest colour first, and build up to darker colours, so that any overprinting is successful.

APRON Spice up teatime with a hand-printed apron.

TABLE RUNNER & NAPKINS Why not revamp a plain table runner and napkins – it will add that something special to a dinner or tea party.

VINTAGE CHAIRS Why not give vintage chairs a new lease of life by recovering them in hand printed fabric. Remove the old material to use as a template. Cut and print your fabric, then simply staple or tack your new fabric into place.

VINTAGE SOFA Once you have mastered screen-printing you may feel ready to take on something on a grander scale. Here we simply printed a large piece of fabric and then gave everything to a professional upholsterer. The upholsterer can advise on how much fabric is required.

STENCILS

The following pages contain seven stencils, which are
ready to use for your own printing and pattern-making.
You can cut them out or copy them as you wish, and
use them to inspire your own designs.

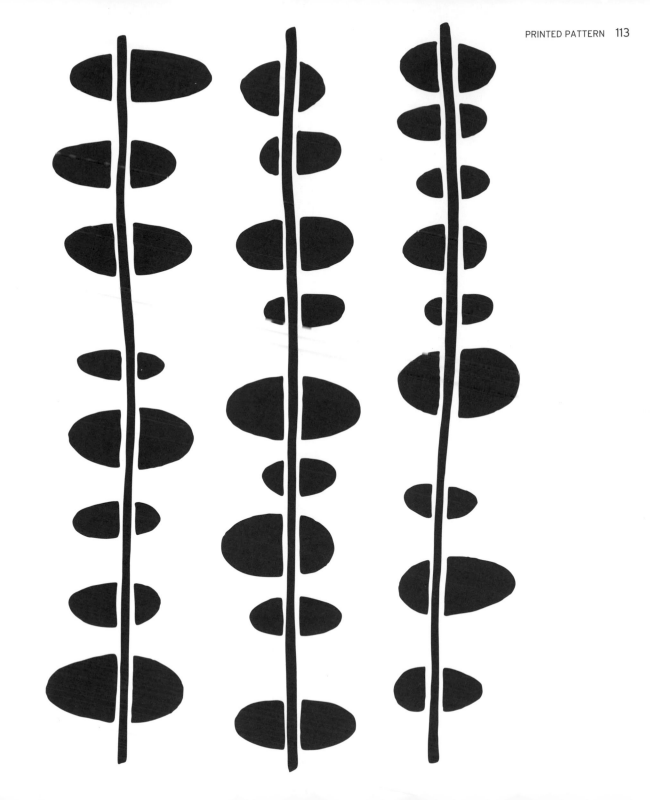

SUPPLIERS

UK

Atlantis Art Materials
7-9 Plumber's Row
London E1 1EQ
www.atlantisart.co.uk
020 7377 8855
Arts, painting and craft supplies

London Graphic Centre
16-18 Shelton St
Covent Garden
London WC2H 9JL
www.londongraphics.co.uk
020 7759 4500
Art, paper and screenprinting
supplies

Pongees
28-30 Hoxton Square
London N1 6NN
www.pongees.co.uk
020 7739 9130
Silk fabrics

R. K. Burt & Company Ltd
57 Union St
London SE1 1SG
www.rkburt.com
020 7407 6474
Art papers

Southfield: The Paper People
25 Hardengreen Industrial Estate
Dalkeith
Midlothian EH22 3NX
Scotland
Paper.people@btconnect.com
0131 654 4300
Paper supplies, envelopes

Fibrecrafts and George Weil
Old Portsmouth Road
Peamarsh
Guildford
Surrey GU3 1LZ
www.georgeweil.co.uk
01483 565 800
Dyes, inks, fabrics and equipment

MacCulloch and Wallis
25-26 Dering Street
London W1S 1AT
www.macculloch-wallis.co.uk
020 8629 0311
Fabrics, haberdashery and trimmings

Colourcraft (C&A) Ltd
Unit 5,
555 Carlisle Street East,
Sheffield S4 8DT
www.colourcraftltd.com
0114 242 1431
Dyes, printing inks, batiks, specialty
inks

Hiva Products
2 Disraeli Street
Aylestone
Leicester LE2 8LX
www.hiva.co.uk
0116 283 6977

Kemtex Educational Suppliers:
Range of Dyes, Inks
Chorley Busines and Technology
Centre and auxillaries
Euxton Lane
Chorley
Lancashire PR7 6TE
www.kemtex.co.uk
01257 230220
Range of dyes, inks and auxillaries

Quality Colours Ltd
Unit 13, Gemini Business Estate
Landmann Way
London SE14 5RL
www.qualitycolours.com
020 7394 8775
Dyeing and printing sundries

Screen Colour Systems
Waterfall
Cottages
Colliers Wood
London SW19 2AE
www.screencoloursystems.co.uk

020 8241 2050
020 8997 1694
Screenprinting equipment, printing
inks

Selectasine Sergraphics Ltd
65 Chislehurst Road
Chisleshurst
Kent BR7 5NP
www.selectasine.com
020 8467 8544
Silkscreens, squeegees, emulsion,
printing inks

Thomas and Vines Ltd
Unit 5 & 6
Sutherland Court
Moor Park Industrial Centre
Tolpits Lane
Watford WD18 9SP
www.flocking.co.uk
01923 775111
Adhesives for fabrics

Tonertex Foils Ltd
PO Box 3746
London N2 9DE
www.tonertex.com
0208 444 1992
Foil papers and glitters

Cornelissen and Son Ltd
105 Great Russell Street
London WC1B 3RY
www.cornellisen.com

020 7636 1045
Printmaking supplies

Daler-Rowney Ltd
Peacock Lane
Bracknell
RG12 8SS
UK
www.daler-rowney.com
t: +44 (0)1344 461000
General art supplies

Paintworks Ltd
99-101 Kingsland Road
London E2 8AG
www.paintworks.biz
020 7729 7451
Art and printmaking supplies, paper

Fred Aldous Ltd
37 Lever Street
Manchester M1 1LW
www.fredaldous.co.uk
0161 236 4224
Art, craft and design supplies

USA

Dick Blick Art Materials
P.O. Box 1267
Galesburg
IL 61402-1267
www.dickblick.com
800 828 4548
Art materials

EZ Screenprint, LLC
P.O. Box 10414
Casa Grande,
AZ 85130
www.ezscreenprint.com
520 423 0409
Screenprinting supplies

Atlantic Papers
1800 Mearns Road, Suite P
Ivyland, PA 18974
www.atlanticpapers.com
800 367 8547
Fine art papers

Pearlpaint
www.pearlpaint.com
1-800-451-7327
Fine art and craft supplies

ACKNOWLEDGMENTS

This book would have never been possible if it was not for our photographer Sophie who spent countless hours trying to capture our vision.

A very special thank you to Lee and Chris for all their hard work, support and advice.

Many thanks to Beejal who helped us with some of our projects.

GLOBALVIEWPOINTS

Gun Control

Christina Fisanick, Book Editor

GREENHAVEN PRESS
A part of Gale, Cengage Learning

GALE
CENGAGE Learning

Detroit • New York • San Francisco • New Haven, Conn • Waterville, Maine • London

GALE
CENGAGE Learning

Christine Nasso, *Publisher*
Elizabeth Des Chenes, *Managing Editor*

© 2010 Greenhaven Press, a part of Gale, Cengage Learning

Gale and Greenhaven Press are registered trademarks used herein under license.

For more information, contact:
Greenhaven Press
27500 Drake Rd.
Farmington Hills, MI 48331-3535
Or you can visit our Internet site at gale.cengage.com

For product information and technology assistance, contact us at

Gale Customer Support, 1-800-877-4253
For permission to use material from this text or product, submit all requests online at www.cengage.com/permissions

Further permissions questions can be emailed to permissionrequest@cengage.com

Articles in Greenhaven Press anthologies are often edited for length to meet page requirements. In addition, original titles of these works are changed to clearly present the main thesis and to explicitly indicate the author's opinion. Every effort is made to ensure that Greenhaven Press accurately reflects the original intent of the authors. Every effort has been made to trace the owners of copyrighted material.

Cover image by Simon Maina/AFP/Getty Images.

LIBRARY OF CONGRESS CATALOGING-IN-PUBLICATION DATA

Gun control / Christina Fisanick, book editor.
    p. cm. -- (Global viewpoints)
    Includes bibliographical references and index.
    ISBN 978-0-7377-4727-0 (hardcover) -- ISBN 978-0-7377-4728-7 (pbk.)
    1. Gun control--Juvenile literature. I. Fisanick, Christina.
    HV7435.G857 2010
    363.33--dc22
                                                            2010000086

Printed in the United States of America
1 2 3 4 5 6 7 14 13 12 11 10

Contents

Chapter 2: Gun Control and Global Crime

Chapter 3: The Effects of Gun Ownership and Gun Control on Society

Chapter 4: The Impact of the Global Arms Trade

Foreword

Global interdependence has become an undeniable reality. Mass media and technology have increased worldwide access to information and created a society of global citizens. Understanding and navigating this global community is a challenge, requiring a high degree of information literacy and a new level of learning sophistication.

Building on the success of its flagship series, *Opposing Viewpoints*, Greenhaven Press has created the *Global Viewpoints* series to examine a broad range of current, often controversial topics of worldwide importance from a variety of international perspectives. Providing students and other readers with the information they need to explore global connections and think critically about worldwide implications, each *Global Viewpoints* volume offers a panoramic view of a topic of widespread significance.

Drugs, famine, immigration—a broad, international treatment is essential to do justice to social, environmental, health, and political issues such as these. Junior high, high school, and early college students, as well as general readers, can all use *Global Viewpoints* anthologies to discern the complexities relating to each issue. Readers will be able to examine unique national perspectives while, at the same time, appreciating the interconnectedness that global priorities bring to all nations and cultures.

Material in each volume is selected from a diverse range of sources, including journals, magazines, newspapers, nonfiction books, speeches, government documents, pamphlets, organization newsletters, and position papers. *Global Viewpoints* is truly global, with material drawn primarily from international sources available in English and secondarily from U.S. sources with extensive international coverage.

Features of each volume in the *Global Viewpoints* series include:

- An **annotated table of contents** that provides a brief summary of each essay in the volume, including the name of the country or area covered in the essay.

- An **introduction** specific to the volume topic.

- A **world map** to help readers locate the countries or areas covered in the essays.

- For each viewpoint, an **introduction** that contains notes about the author and source of the viewpoint explains why material from the specific country is being presented, summarizes the main points of the viewpoint, and offers three **guided reading questions** to aid in understanding and comprehension.

- **For further discussion** questions that promote critical thinking by asking the reader to compare and contrast aspects of the viewpoints or draw conclusions about perspectives and arguments.

- A worldwide list of **organizations to contact** for readers seeking additional information.

- A **periodical bibliography** for each chapter and a **bibliography of books** on the volume topic to aid in further research.

- A comprehensive **subject index** to offer access to people, places, events, and subjects cited in the text, with the countries covered in the viewpoints highlighted.

Global Viewpoints is designed for a broad spectrum of readers who want to learn more about current events, history, political science, government, international relations, economics, environmental science, world cultures, and sociology—students doing research for class assignments or debates, teachers and faculty seeking to supplement course materials, and others wanting to understand current issues better. By presenting how people in various countries perceive the root causes, current consequences, and proposed solutions to worldwide challenges, *Global Viewpoints* volumes offer readers opportunities to enhance their global awareness and their knowledge of cultures worldwide.

Introduction

> "Contrary to other trafficked and deadly
> commodities such as narcotics, small
> arms usually begin their life legally."
>
> Nicolas Florquin,
> "The Illicit Trade in Small
> Arms and Light Weapons,"
> IIAS Newsletter, Fall 2006

Although guns and the use of gun powder can be traced back to the 1200s, everyday citizens did not possess them until the late 1400s. Given the incredible power of guns to maim and kill humans as well as animals, it is not surprising that restrictions were placed on firearms early in their history. However, gun control regulations and debates surrounding them did not become prominent throughout the world until the end of the 1800s, when small arms became cheaper to manufacture and global trade encouraged their proliferation.

Gun control comes in many forms. Gun ownership registration cards have been required by many countries for decades, including Nazi-era Germany. Other types of gun control include background checks and mandatory firearm safety classes as are required in the Czech Republic and the United States. Some countries, like Mexico, limit gun ownership to hunting and self-defense, thereby banning private citizens from owning certain types of weapons, including some handguns and automatic weapons. The strictest form of gun control includes an outright ban of all guns, such as was first instituted in 1930s China.

Worldwide gun control efforts ebb and flow with history and in relation to other cultural changes. For example, it is not unusual for gun control laws to be amended before, during, and after a world war. In *Guns and Violence*, Joyce Lee

Malcolm notes that gun laws in England became more restrictive after World War II. In addition, there are instances throughout history of citizens being disarmed after being conquered by dictators. For instance, on August 29, 1588, Toyotomi Hideyoshi, a peasant who had overthrown the Japanese government, announced "the Sword Hunt," which banned the possession of swords and firearms by the non-noble classes. Stephen Turnbull writes in *The Samurai: A Military History* that "Hideyoshi's resources were such that the edict was carried out to the letter."

Anti-gun control activists look to this example as proof that guns can be a powerful means of defense against a tyrannical government. These gun proponents often cite historical instances, such as Joseph Stalin's gun confiscation program that began in the Soviet Union in 1929, as evidence. According to Aaron Zelman, executive director of Jews for the Preservation of Firearms Ownership (JPFO), the introduction of gun control has foreshadowed the emergence of oppressive regimes throughout the twentieth century, including Pol Pot, the leader of Cambodia in the 1970s. However, not everyone is convinced that gun control leads to tyrannical control. Jessica Henig of FactCheckEd.org argues that "We have no doubt that Stalin, Hitler and Pol Pot tried to keep guns out of the hands of ordinary citizens. But that doesn't mean that gun control necessarily leads to totalitarian dictatorships."

Nonetheless, many gun rights supporters assert that taking guns away from the people can lead to serious ramifications, including genocide. The Jewish Holocaust during World War II is the most prominent example cited in opposition to gun control laws. In the June 2001 issue of *American Rifleman*, Stephen P. Halbrook acknowledges that "Night of Broken Glass," or "Kristallnacht," the infamous Nazi rampage against Germany's Jews, was successful because "resistance was hampered by the lack of civilian arms possession." All persons of Jewish descent were forced to give up their firearms by Nazi decree in 1938. What followed Kristallnacht was the mass genocide of 6 million Jews. Halbrook further states, "As this century has shown, terrorist governments have the capacity to commit genocide against millions of people, provided that the people are unarmed."

Supporters of stricter gun laws disagree with the relationship between civilian arms possession and the prevention of genocide. For example, the perpetrators of the Rwandan genocide, which ended in 1994, mostly used machetes, not guns, to kill eight hundred thousand of their relatives and neighbors. There is no direct proof that civilian gun ownership would have prevented or even reduced the number of injuries and deaths during the genocide. In fact, if more people had access to firearms, there would likely have been more deaths, according to the World Health Organization (WHO), which supports stricter gun laws.

Perhaps the most common events that promote a resurgence in gun control activities are mass shootings. Mass shootings around the world have prompted gun rights opponents to call for stricter gun laws. Perhaps the most well known of such instances is the Port Arthur massacre in Tasmania, Australia, in 1996. On that day, Martin Bryant shot and killed thirty-five people. In the aftermath of this killing spree, Australian officials implemented a ban on the sale of all automatic and semiautomatic weapons and began a gun buyback program. According to Orietta Guerrera in a 2006 article that appeared in Australia's the *Age*, about 660,000 automatic and semiautomatic rifles were handed in under the 1996 national buyback scheme. Although some hunting and shooting organizations were against the new laws, they were passed largely because of the fear of future mass shootings.

Despite strict gun laws, mass shootings do occur. Gun rights activists point to the recent school shooting in Germany as an example of how stricter gun laws do not lead to a safer society. Germany has some of the most stringent gun laws in the world. Handguns can only be purchased by people over the age of eighteen and more lethal weapons are sold only to those over the age of twenty-one. In addition, firearms can be purchased only after the buyer has obtained a license, granted after a thorough background check. These regulations did not stop seventeen-year-old student, Tim Kretschmer, from killing fifteen of his former classmates at a school in Stuttgart. Luke Harding, in a 2009 article in the *Guardian*, notes that Kretschmer's family kept eighteen different weapons at home.

Given that the trade of small arms—legal and illicit—is big business throughout the world, it is no wonder that efforts to control firearms have been met with fierce opposition by some. According to the Stockholm International Peace Research Institute (SIPRI), in 2006 the combined arms sales of the top one hundred largest arms-producing companies totaled an estimated $315 billion. That number does not account for the estimated $2–10 billion made each year by the illicit trade of firearms around the globe, which has been documented by many worldwide organizations, including the International Action Network on Small Arms (IANSA). According to Lora Lumpe in a 2003 article in Amnesty International's magazine, "The governments of the United States and other countries, including China and Russia, see new regulation as limiting their commercial and foreign policy options, while arms manufacturers see a threat to their bottom line."

It is doubtful that the world will ever be gun-free, and in fact, many people argue that it is the right of all citizens to bear arms. The authors in *Global Viewpoints: Gun Control* debate current views on gun control in the following chapters: Gun Control Policies Around the World, Gun Control and Global Crime, The Effects of Gun Ownership and Gun Control on Society, and The Impact of the Global Arms Trade.

The only aspect of this international debate that is certain is that firearms and laws surrounding them will continue to take center stage for many years to come.

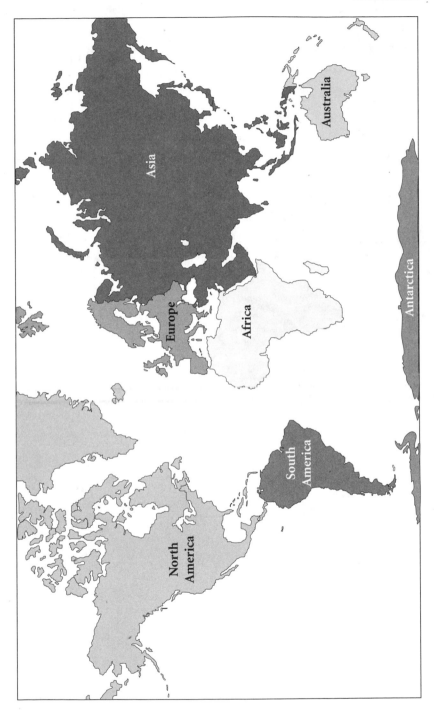

CHAPTER 1

Gun Control Policies Around the World

Switzerland Considers Gun Control

Imogen Foulkes

Imogen Foulkes is a regular contributor to BBC News and other international news publications. In the following viewpoint, she reports on talks amongst the Swiss people on the long-standing tradition of arming its citizenry through mandatory military service. High rates of suicide and domestic violence involving firearms have prompted the Swiss government to reconsider the requirement that all men keep guns and ammunition in their homes. However, many citizens have balked at these proposed changes, arguing that learning to use a gun is a rite of passage for Swiss men.

As you read, consider the following questions:

1. What do Swiss men take home with them following military service, according to Foulkes?
2. As noted by Foulkes, what is the only other country that has a higher rate of suicide than Switzerland?
3. Which European country has the highest rate of gun-related domestic violence, as cited by Foulkes?

Switzerland's the only country that requires its soldiers to keep guns at home. But concerns over high suicide rates and killings within families have caused some to ask whether having them there is simply too dangerous.

Imogen Foulkes, "Switzerland Considers Gun Control," *Deutsche Welle*, July 29, 2007, pp. 1–3. Reproduced by permission. http://www.dw-world.de.

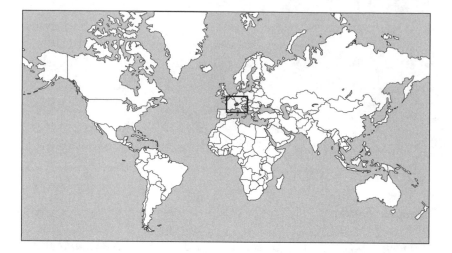

All Swiss men must do military service—they all learn to shoot—and when they go home, they take their assault rifles and 50 rounds of ammunition with them.

"For me it's just routine," said Philippe Schaub, heading home after his latest stint in the army. "We all do military service, we're all given a gun to take home. I keep it in my cupboard just like the coats and the snowboard and the vacuum cleaner."

The idea is to have an army ready for call-up anytime. Although neutral Switzerland hasn't fought a war for centuries, Christophe Keckeis, chief of the armed forces, said he sees no reason for change.

"The policy is that every single soldier has his weapon at home, a pistol or a gun," Keckeis said.

"The idea is to have an army ready for call-up at anytime."

"This is a very robust tradition," he added. "We do have enormous confidence in our men, we know they are well-educated, and we are 100 percent sure that they know how to deal with this weapon and the ammunition."

High Rates of Suicide and Domestic Violence

But not everyone shares that confidence. Tanja Vollenweider had a happy family life until four years ago. She and her husband had just bought a new house. He was between jobs, so they had a few money worries, but not, she thought, big ones.

"It was a normal, happy day, we had taken the kids to the zoo, we had people to dinner in the evening," Vollenweider said. "In the middle of the night my daughter woke me—she said my husband had run out of the house with his army gun. I tried to run after him, but I was too late."

Vollenweider's husband killed himself.

The only country with a higher rate of suicide with guns than Switzerland is the United States. And it's not just suicide: Every month or so, a Swiss man turns his gun on his family. The country has the highest rate of domestic violence using guns in Europe.

"These deaths that are happening, these slaughters, these murders, are terrible, but there's much more to the problem than that," said Sabin Bieri, a professor of gender politics at the University of Berne, who is part of a growing campaign to get the guns out of Swiss homes. "The weapon is a constant threat in family life in Switzerland, which I think is such a terrible thing for many women and many children."

"Learning to use a gun has been a rite of passage for young Swiss men for centuries."

Subject to Referendum

But it's hard to challenge tradition. Learning to use a gun has been a rite of passage for young Swiss men for centuries.

Keckeis sees proposals to take the guns away as a threat to the masculinity of his troops.

23

Swiss Gun Figures

- Estimations of the number of firearms in circulation in Switzerland range upwards from 1.2 million....

- Army-issue weapons are said to be involved in the deaths of more than 300 people in Switzerland every year.

- According to Ipsilon Suicide Prevention, 34% of suicides among men are due to firearms, compared with only 3.7% of female suicides.

- An international survey, carried out by the European Alliance Against Depression and published last year [2008], found that almost half of all suicides by Swiss youngsters were committed using a gun.

Swissinfo.ch,
"Move to Ban Gun Rifles at Home Gathers Space,"
February 24, 2009. www.swissinfo.ch.

"They will really be taken as unserious men," he said. "It would be a sign that we don't have confidence in them any more, after being so confident for many years, and they would be really lost. It would be a signal that the political power in Switzerland is no longer confident in its armed forces and in its population."

Those political considerations aren't much comfort to Tanja Vollenweider. She's convinced she would still have her husband if the gun hadn't been so readily available.

"This only happened because the gun was right here at home," she said. "My husband wouldn't have gone out looking for one. If the gun hadn't been here I think he'd still be alive."

Little by little, there are signs that the Swiss may be ready for change: This summer [2007], left-wing parties will launch plans for a nationwide referendum to force the army to take the weapons away.

The process will take awhile but the current generation of new conscripts may be among the last to take their guns home with them.

South Africa's Gun-Free Zone Policies Have Been Effective

Adèle Kirsten et al.

Adèle Kirsten is the former director of Gun Free South Africa and is currently an advisory board member for the United Kingdom's Armed Violence and Poverty Initiative. Along with her colleagues, in the following viewpoint, she argues that the establishment of gun-free zones (GFZs) throughout South Africa has reduced firearm crimes and other related casualties. Given South Africa's history of armed violence, GFZs provide an opportunity to galvanize local communities in the fight against gun crimes.

As you read, consider the following questions:

1. What are some areas that have been established as gun-free zones?

2. According to the authors, how did townships typically define "youth" during apartheid?

3. How many firearms are currently owned by South African civilians?

O n 27 April 1994, millions of South Africans cast their votes in the country's first fully democratic general elections, signalling an end to more than 350 years of political

Adèle Kirsten et al., *Island of Safety in a Sea of Guns: Gun-Free Zones in South Africa's Fothane, Diepkloof, and Khayelitsha*, Geneva, Switzerland: Small Arms Survey, 2006. Copyright © 2006 Graduate Institute of International Studies, Geneva. All rights reserved. Reproduced by permission.

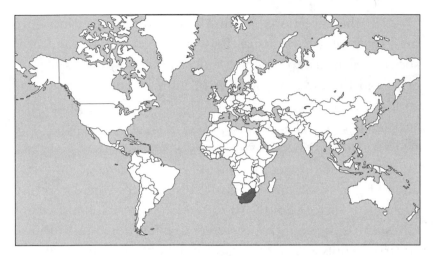

rule by a white minority over the black majority. South Africa's history is one of colonial conquest, dispossession, segregation, and repression; one in which firearms played an important role in maintaining the border between the oppressed and the oppressor, between the colonized and the colonizer. With the state's implementation of apartheid policies after 1948, which further entrenched white rule, the military expanded its influence into all areas of social life, becoming a pervasive element in South African society. In response to the increased repression by the apartheid state, resistance organizations turned to armed violence as one strand in the strategy for national liberation. Many members of the military-wing of the African National Congress (ANC) regarded themselves as soldiers fighting in a people's war. Although many held that South Africa was at war, it was generally accepted that the conflict was a low-level civil war, commonly referred to as 'low-intensity conflict'. As a result of several factors, such as internal mass mobilization against apartheid and increasing international pressure for a political solution to the South African conflict, negotiations for a new political dispensation started in 1990, culminating in a democratic constitution and the 1994 elections.

After these elections, South Africa continued to experience high levels of gun violence. Religious organizations and civil society began to express their concern that easy access to firearms and the excessive number of guns in South Africa constituted one of the biggest threats to the fledgling multiracial society. The response to this threat was the emergence of a national gun-free movement in South Africa.

A major component of this social movement was the creation of gun-free zones (GFZs)—social spaces where guns are prohibited—across South Africa. Today, there are hundreds of GFZs across the country. These are in educational institutions, such as schools and universities; churches; community centres; health facilities, such as hospitals and local community clinics; NGOs [nongovernmental organizations]; taverns and *shebeens* (unlicensed bars); banks; corporate buildings; local, provincial, and national government buildings; and in some public spaces such as sports stadiums. GFZs emerged, not just as a response to the high levels of armed violence that had marked the four years of negotiations prior to the 1994 general elections, but also because of people's experience of decades of structural and state-sponsored violence during the apartheid era.

This report looks both at the process whereby GFZs were set up and at the impact they have had to date. Quantitative data such as crime and firearms data, as well as a GFZ audit carried out in 2000, provide some broad insights, particularly at the national level. The qualitative data represents the more important part of this assessment because it highlights the nuanced processes and diverse impact of GFZs within different social contexts, identifying some of their unintended consequences. This qualitative data was gathered from three case studies in three provinces: Fothane in Mapela district, Limpopo Province; Diepkloof in Soweto, Gauteng Province; and Khayelitsha in the Cape Town metropolitan area, Western Cape Province. The case studies involved in-depth interviews and focus group discussions. The three sites were chosen because all of them were known to have set up some form of GFZs in response to requests from community leaders to assist both in reducing gun violence and in creating a safer environment.

Study Outcomes

The study draws the following conclusions.

The flexibility of the GFZ process means that GFZs are implemented in a variety of forms depending on local needs and context. This enables anyone to declare his or her premises a GFZ, making it difficult to determine the exact number of GFZs in South Africa. Although the proliferation of guns is an indicator of historic and current levels of violent conflict in South African society, GFZs are indicators of the commitment to an alternative vision of a peaceful social order. GFZs can be important innovations that play a critical role in some communities, enhancing social cohesion and providing residents with a tangible means through which to express their commitment to a more safe and secure society.

"[Gun-free zones] are indicators of the commitment to an alternative vision of a peaceful social order."

GFZs give people feelings of increased security and lead to real increases in safety, primarily, but not exclusively, within the GFZ venue. This was most evident in the reported reduction of gunshots heard across all three case studies. This does not necessarily mean a direct reduction in the number of guns either in circulation or in use, but rather is an indication of how GFZs contribute to increased feelings of safety. This may primarily be influenced by the process of actively engaging in crime-prevention interventions, thereby empowering residents to do something about violence in their communities. In one particular community, the reported reduction in the number of gunshot victims presenting at a health facility and the reduction in the public carrying of firearms were further examples of the positive impact of GFZs.

Given the proliferation of firearms in contemporary South Africa, these 'islands of safety' may allow maximum grassroots participation in building more secure social arenas. The GFZ vision has been successful in mobilizing individuals and communities across South Africa to challenge gun ownership as normative behaviour and in support of the vision of a society in which people are free from the fear of gun violence. But the success of GFZs has been uneven and their impact limited because of several factors, such as the climate of crime and the high demand for guns, as well as the lack of resources and insufficient attention given to involving all role players in a participatory process during implementation of GFZs.

In almost all areas, regardless of context, the GFZ project has had a positive impact at the individual level. It has changed individuals' lives: In some instances it has given people, mostly young unemployed men, an opportunity to play a role in contributing to a more secure environment within their immediate communities. It has also given them meaning and status in their communities. The GFZ project has contributed to other violence-reduction projects such as the Centre for the Study of Violence and Reconciliation's 40 schools project combined with the Tiisa Thuto project in Soweto. These projects have contributed to a climate where guns are seen as unacceptable in some public spaces such as schools.

The GFZ project had a direct influence on the provision of firearm-free Zone (FFZs) in the Firearms Control Act (FCA) of 2000, which was largely attributable to the innovative and public nature of the GFZ campaign. There have been long delays in finalizing the regulations attached to this act, which were only completed in mid-2004, with the law coming into effect in July of that year. There has, therefore, not been a lot of practical experience with the law, and none that could be discussed in this [viewpoint].

An inclusive and participatory process in the implementation of GFZs is key to their success. This is further enhanced by the presence of well-trained and well-motivated local community activists with good communication strategies enacted through the use of materials and workshops. Realizing the potential of GFZs depends on socially inclusive processes conducted in socially cohesive communities.

People expressed their dissatisfaction and frustration at the lack of standardized implementation and enforcement procedures, which they regarded as weakening the potential of the project. The lack of a systematic enforcement policy or practice, which includes communication about the GFZ status of a particular area, weakens its impact and can lead to feelings of insecurity within the GFZ site. This contributes to the GFZ sign losing its meaning and capacity to challenge the norms of public gun carrying.

GFZs' potential is not always realized because of the weakness and limited resources of the gun-free movement, in the sense of a grassroots mobilization against the proliferation of firearms, led by Gun Free South Africa (GFSA), at both the local and national levels. GFZs require high maintenance in the sense that for the gun-free sign to sustain its meaning and impact, residents need ongoing input and information on the gun debates in the country, not just on GFZs. This requires high levels of energy and resources, which raises a question about the sustainability of GFZs and therefore also of their replicability, either within the country or elsewhere. . . .

The History of Violence in South Africa

South Africa has inherited a 'culture of violence' embodied both in the violence of colonialism and apartheid, and a romanticization of the armed struggle and mythologizing of the AK-47 assault rifle. Guns have always been a feature of life in South Africa, especially over the last 50 years: whether they were small arms and light weapons distributed by the apart-

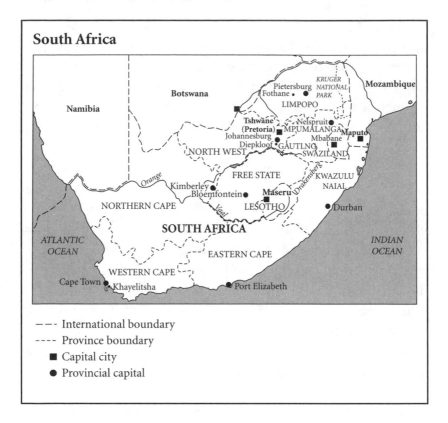

South Africa

- – – International boundary
- - - - Province boundary
- ■ Capital city
- ● Provincial capital

heid government to the young white conscripts used to defend the nation, or those in the hands of the white commandos spread throughout the country as the civilian-military arm of apartheid state protection, or those issued to the police and security forces of the semiautonomous black homelands.

The response of members of the anti-apartheid liberation movements to this highly militarized and well-armed state and citizenry was to arm themselves, and so, especially in the latter years of apartheid, weapons in the hands of the country's black youth—as members of self-defence or self-protection units—became more common. This led to the generic term 'youth' being used in the townships to describe young men and women between the ages of 15 and 25. The term came to signify a culturally and politically separate identity, often associated with violence. Guns have also been an 'important weapon in maintaining the border between the oppressed and the oppressor, between the colonized and the colonizer'. The perceived masculine identity of colonizer and gun owner reinforced the racial dimension of gun ownership in South Africa, where, for most of the apartheid era, private firearm ownership was restricted to whites only. In the new dispensation, therefore, for some black South Africans, owning a firearm is thus one expression of having attained full citizenship rights under the new democratic government. This means that in the current context guns are highly related to race and linked to a militarized conception of citizenship.

South Africa experienced high levels of armed violence during the four years of the negotiated settlement (1990–94). Guns were no longer just in the hands of the state and became increasingly available across all sectors of society, altering the nature of conflicts in the home and within and between communities. This legacy of violence continues to affect the new economic, social, and political relations being forged in South Africa's relatively recent post-apartheid democracy. . . .

"South Africa has inherited a 'culture of violence' embodied both in the violence of colonialism and apartheid."

Firearms Ownership and Murder Rates

South Africa is a heavily armed society. In 1994 there were 3.5 million licensed firearms in the hands of 2.4 million individuals. Although licensed firearms ownership has increased in the last ten years, the rate of firearms ownership applications has slowed down considerably. South African civilians now own 3.7 million firearms, while the police and the army have 567,000 guns between them. South African civilians thus have more than six times as many firearms as those held by the state security forces. In 1994, there were 26,832 murders in South Africa, of which 11,134 were committed with firearms. This equates to 28.8 firearms murders per 100,000 people. Although the number of murders in South Africa since 1994 has declined, the percentage of people killed by firearms increased from 41 per cent of all murders in 1994 to 49.3 per cent in 2000.

"South Africa is a heavily armed society."

Most of the firearms are owned by men—whether in state structures, such as the police force or the military; for leisure or sport activities such as hunting; or for self-defence in the home. Likewise, the majority of firearms murder victims in South Africa are men. In 2003, 27.9 per cent of the 22,248 non-natural deaths recorded that year were firearms-related. For every female death from violence and injury, 4.4 male deaths were reported. Of the 17,932 male fatalities in 2003, the leading external cause of death was firearms at 31 per cent. Deaths attributed to violence and suicide are particularly high in the 15–44 year age group, peaking in the 25–29 year age group.

Crime statistics show a significant drop in several violent crime categories. For example, murders peaked in 1995 at 26,877, staying at roughly this level for several years. Since 2000, the murder rate has been decreasing each year, with a total of 19,824 murders recorded in 2003–04. This represents a drop of more than 23 per cent since 1994. Despite this decrease, an average of 54 people are murdered every day in South Africa. Since 2000, no breakdown of the murder figures has been released by type of weapon/cause of death. However, 11,176 murders were committed with guns in 2000 and there were more than 21,000 attempted firearms murders. The data shows a decrease in actual numbers but an increase in the ratio of gun-use to other murder weapons, both for murders committed with guns and for attempted firearms murders. In both the murder and attempted murder categories for 2000, handguns (pistols or revolvers) were the most commonly used weapons, with assault rifles used in 151 murder cases. Armed robbery (a category that covers firearms and other weapons) reached a high of 88,178 cases in 2000. Another firearms-related offence relevant to this study, and which is high compared to other countries for the period for which statistics are available (1994–2000), is that of 'pointing of a firearm'. There have always been at least 20,000 such offences reported per year, peaking in 2000 at 27,933. The significance of this offence is that it demonstrates how firearms are often part of threatening behaviour in South Africa.

Jamaican Gun Control Policies Are Ineffective

Denton Tyndale

In the following viewpoint, Jamaican native and gun ownership advocate Denton Tyndale argues that Jamaican gun laws should be less restrictive. He asserts that the people of Jamaica are not barbarians who would murder each other over minor disputes. Instead, he urges lawmakers to reconsider the current gun laws to allow more Jamaicans to arm themselves against intruders. Tyndale notes that an armed populace of law-abiding citizens will limit the responsibility of the police force and will deter crime.

As you read, consider the following questions:

1. For how long has Jamaica enforced gun control laws?
2. On average, how many guns are there per one hundred people in Jamaica?
3. About how many officers make up the domestic security force in Jamaica?

All Jamaican crime plans will fail until they recognise that the Jamaican citizens (being defenceless prey against criminal men and women who will "never" be stripped of their illegal arms) must be empowered to help in the fight against violent crime. It's not the job of the police to prevent

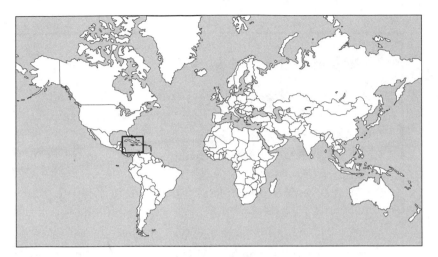

armed robberies, burglary, home invasions, rapes and murders and, frankly, no reasonable person could call on the 10,000 police and 3,000 soldiers to be instantly available to protect each of the 2.8 million citizens against these things. A criminal in your home can reach you in a few seconds.

Could the police reach you faster if you call them? What if you live in a remote area or somewhere isolated? How fast could help arrive? Running away is not always an option. The elderly and people with disabilities, for the most part, simply do not have the option. Running away might also save your skin, but it won't save the loved ones you protect for which you have a responsibility to shelter from harm.

Gun Control Does Not Work

Jamaica has had more than 34 years of experience with gun control and we can say resoundingly that it does not work. The cries of "get those guns" are cries of mass hysteria and shared delusions. The American military and [U.S.] Coast Guard have been unable to prevent most contraband from entering their shores. How can we expect our security forces to prevent all illegal guns from entering our island? For all the hundreds of guns that are recovered by the police each year,

Gun Crimes in Jamaica

The island of 2.7m [million] people, which is slightly smaller than Connecticut, has one of the highest murder rates in the world.

The figures are chilling—there were 1,674 murders in 2005, up from 1,471 murders the year before. Last year [2006], the number of murders came down to 1,340.

So far this year, there have been about 300 murders.

The never-ending spiral of gun crime has led to a vicious cycle of killings on both sides—nearly a dozen policemen have been killed on duty this year alone, and civil rights groups allege that the police have also been trigger happy.

Soutik Biswas,
"Jamaica Struggles to Fight Crime,"
BBC News, May 16, 2007.

there are hundreds more that have not been detected. The criminal gunmen will always have guns. Leaving good people defenceless against violent criminals who have shown their commitment to taking lives is a sin.

To those who would say that Jamaicans are barbarians who cannot be entrusted with guns because they are incapable of resolving their disputes amicably, I would call those people bigots, classists, elitists and possibly even racists. Jamaicans are not an inferior people. If Jamaicans were so hotheaded and incapable of resolving disputes peacefully, we would see the masses hacking each other to death with machetes or any other weapons at their disposal. Jamaicans are not murderers by nature. It is the criminal scum who are in the minority with nationwide notoriety who have given us that false no-tion. Jamaicans—the majority of which are peace-loving rural folk—condemn violence. Let us not use bigoted arguments to prevent good people from having effective means of self-defence.

When guns are outlawed, only outlaws will have guns.

"Jamaicans—the majority of which are peace-loving rural folk—condemn violence."

Why do I do this? By encouraging others to become able to defend themselves effectively, I also gain personal security. A defenceless population is an easy target for crime. A population that can defend itself is not.

Facts About Gun Ownership

1. Self-defence is a right. You have a right to life as declared by the UN's [Universal] Declaration of Human Rights, but how can you enforce your right to life if you have no "effective" means to defend it?

2. Guns are inanimate objects. They do not have a mind of their own. They are tools that do the bidding of the person manipulating them. Guns are legal in Jamaica and you can receive a permit for the firearms that you own. The problem is that there is still some amount of elitism where issuing of permits is concerned. A person must be considered worthy before the state allows him to have a permit to obtain a firearm.

3. Licensed firearms are practically never used in committing crimes. All permit holders in Jamaica are required to do a ballistics test before they receive the firearm permit. If they try to use their gun in a crime, the police will immediately know who did it and come to the person's house and arrest him. It is unlikely that such a licensed firearm holder would commit

a crime anyway. To receive a permit, you must not have had a criminal conviction . . . law-abiding citizens are just that: law-abiding.

"A person must be considered worthy before the state allows him to have a permit to obtain a firearm."

---

4. Criminals don't use licensed firearms to commit crimes. Their guns are high-powered weapons smuggled in from all over. It's already illegal to obtain and carry a gun without a permit, but criminals don't care because they don't respect laws. Result? They carry guns anyway (without permits) and often turn them on innocents.

5. Criminals prefer unarmed victims. They are so bold in Jamaica because they really do not expect anybody to return fire. This is why one guy can enter a bar and order everybody to get flat and proceed to execute five people as happened in Bog Walk in 2007. In Jamaica, there are about three guns per 100 persons.

6. Laws that take guns away from law-abiding citizens embolden and help criminals. Or: When guns are outlawed, only outlaws will have guns.

7. Do you believe that you will ever face a violent situation? Will you or a family member ever be raped? Will you or a loved one ever be mugged? Will somebody try to enter your home? Hoping that it doesn't happen to you is not a survival solution. If any of these things happened (God forbid), would you think:

    a. These men are disobeying laws that prohibit them from carrying firearms.

    b. I wish the police were here right now.

    c. I wish I had pepper spray.

    d. I wish I had a gun.

8. Gun control—the act of taking away firearms from law-abiding citizens or making it more difficult for them to obtain—has never been demonstrated to lower crime rates anywhere. In fact, gun control has been linked to increases in violent crimes. How strange? No. It's actually common sense. Law-abiding citizens are just that. They are law-abiding. They don't plan crimes. They use their guns for self-defence. Criminals get guns any way you take it. You can't stop criminals from getting guns as we see by the numerous firearms recovered by the police. If you take away the means of defending themselves from law-abiding citizens then already armed criminals will find it easier to have their way with them.

9. Many people are capable of living in harmony with each other. Psychopaths and other antisocial individuals lack the very things that enable you to cooperate in society. They are intraspecies predators who delight in causing others suffering. There is no reforming them and they simply do not understand mercy. Think about the murders of babies, women and the elderly in this country that seem almost never to have a point. Predators are intent on using violence. Will you let them?

10. The state is not your nanny. The police are not under any obligation to risk their lives to save yours. The police carry firearms including fully automatic rifles to defend their lives. There are about 13,000 members of the security forces, 10,000 of which are police and 3,000 of which are soldiers. They cannot prevent crime from happening to 2.8 million people. Their function is to gather evidence by examining the bodies of victims for clues and possibly use those clues to locate and arrest suspects.

Imagine: You decide to apply for a firearm permit. The government issues you a firearm permit. You purchase a gun and the ballistics test is done on it so that the police can identify your firearm whenever it is used in any kind of shooting. With your new firearm, would you:

a. hold up the nearest business.

b. go after your enemies and shoot them.

c. remain the law-abiding citizen that you are.

d. be even more polite than before since you really want to avoid conflicts of any kind.

Jamaica crime plan? Let us have GUNS!

India's Gun Control Policies Are Ineffective

Abhijeet Singh

In the following viewpoint, Abhijeet Singh, a technology expert and writer for Greatech, a computer consulting firm, argues that gun control laws in India are ineffective, in part because they are rooted during a time when India was under British colonial rule. By tracing current firearms laws back to the Indian Arms Act of 1878, he explains how they are outdated and not an accurate reflection of India's current attitudes about gun ownership. Arming the people of India, asserts Singh, will reduce violent crime and curtail India's involvement in the small arms trade.

As you read, consider the following questions:

1. What is the Indian Arms Act, 1878, according to the author?
2. Annually, what percentage of gun owners in the United States use firearms to commit crimes?
3. More people in India are killed in what type of accidents than firearm accidents?

I live in India and I am a proud firearm owner—but I am the exception not the norm, an odd situation in a country with a proud martial heritage and a long history of firearm innovation. This is not because the people of India are averse

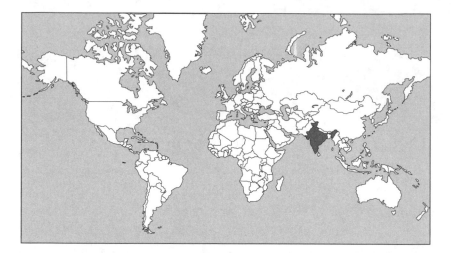

to gun ownership, but instead due to Draconian anti-gun legislation going back to colonial times.

Colonial Era Gun Laws

To trace the roots of India's anti-gun legislation we need to step back to the latter half of the 19th century. The British had recently fought off a major Indian rebellion (the mutiny of 1857) and were busy putting in place measures to ensure that the events of 1857 were never repeated. These measures included a major restructuring of administration and the colonial British Indian Army along with improvements in communications and transportation. Meanwhile the Indian masses were systematically being disarmed and the means of local firearm production destroyed, to ensure that they (the Indian masses) would never again have the means to rise in rebellion against their colonial masters. Towards this end the colonial government, under Lord Lytton as Viceroy (1874–1880), brought into existence the Indian Arms Act, 1878 (11 of 1878), an act which exempted Europeans and ensured that no Indian could possess a weapon of any description unless the British masters considered him a "loyal" subject of the British Empire.

[A quote from James Burgh, as] an example of British thinking in colonial times:

"No kingdom can be secured otherwise than by arming the people. The possession of arms is the distinction between a freeman and a slave. He, who has nothing, and who himself belongs to another, must be defended by him, whose property he is, and needs no arms. But he, who thinks he is his own master, and has what he can call his own, ought to have arms to defend himself, and what he possesses; else he lives precariously, and at discretion."

"Meanwhile the Indian masses were systematically being disarmed and the means of local firearm production destroyed."

And thoughts (on this subject) of the man who wanted to rule the world [Adolf Hitler]:

"The most foolish mistake we could possibly make would be to allow the subject races to possess arms. History shows that all conquerors who have allowed the subject races to carry arms have prepared their own downfall by so doing. Indeed, I would go so far as to say that the supply of arms to the underdogs is a sine qua non [essential] for the overthrow of any sovereignty."

The leaders of our freedom struggle recognised this; even Gandhi the foremost practitioner of passive resistance and nonviolence had this to say about the British policy of gun control in India:

"Among the many misdeeds of the British rule in India, history will look upon the act depriving a whole nation of arms, as the blackest."

Postindependence

India became independent in 1947, but it still took 12 years before this act was finally repealed. In 1959 the British era Indian Arms Act, 1878 (11 of 1878) was finally consigned to history and a new act, the Arms Act, 1959 was enacted. This was later supplemented by the Arms Rules, 1962. Unfortunately this new legislation was also formulated based on the Indian government's innate distrust of its own citizens. Though somewhat better than the British act, this legislation gave vast arbitrary powers to the "Licensing Authorities", in effect ensuring that it is often difficult and sometimes impossible for an ordinary law-abiding Indian citizen to procure an arms license.

> "A system of licensing and registration is the perfect device to deny gun ownership to the bourgeoise."
>
> —*Vladimir Ilyich Lenin*

Also the policy of throttling private arms manufacturing was continued even after independence. Limits on the quantity and type of arms that could be produced by private manufacturers were placed—ensuring that the industry could never hope to be globally competitive and was instead consigned to producing cheap shotguns, of mostly indifferent quality, in small quantities. A citizen wishing to purchase a decent firearm depended solely on imports, which were a bit more expensive but vastly superior in quality.

This changed towards the mid to late 1980s, when the government, citing domestic insurgency as the reason, put a complete stop to all small arms imports. The fact that there is no documented evidence of any terrorists ever having used licensed weapons to commit an act of terror on Indian soil seems to be of no consequence to our government. The prices of (legal and licensed) imported weapons have been on an upward spiral ever since—beating the share market and gold in terms of pure return on investment. Even the shoddy domestically produced guns suddenly seem to have found a market.

Also since the government now had a near monopoly on (even half-way decent) arms and ammunition for the civilian market, they started turning the screws by pricing their crude public-sector products (ammunition, rifles, shotguns and small quantities of handguns) at ridiculously high rates—products that frankly, given a choice no one would ever purchase.

> "That rifle on the wall of the labourer's cottage or working-class flat is the symbol of democracy. It is our job to see that it stays there."
>
> —*George Orwell, the author of* Animal Farm *and* 1984, *himself a Socialist*

Why Citizens Need to Be Armed

Curtailing gun ownership, to curb violent crime, through denying licenses or making legal arms and ammunition ridiculously expensive is based on flawed reasoning. The fact is that licensed firearms are found to be used in a statistically insignificant number of violent crimes— motorcycles and cars are far more dangerous. The certainty that a potential victim is unarmed is an encouragement to armed criminals. Less guns, more crime. Most violent crimes involving firearms are committed using untraceable illegal guns. Terrorists or the Mafia are not going to be deterred by gun control laws; they will be willing and able to procure arms of their choice and use them to commit crimes irrespective of any laws. Ironically, in India it is cheaper (by several times) to buy the same gun in the black market than it is to buy it legally!

"Ironically, in India it is cheaper (by several times) to buy the same gun in the black market than it is to buy it legally!"

"Gun control? It's the best thing you can do for crooks and gangsters. I want you to have nothing. If I'm a bad guy, I'm always gonna have a gun. Safety locks? You'll pull the trigger with a lock on, and I'll pull the trigger. We'll see who wins."

—*Sammy "The Bull" Gravano, Mafia hit man*

"The supposed quietude of a good man allures the ruffian; while on the other hand, arms, like laws, discourage and keep the invader and the plunderer in awe, and preserve order in the world as well as property. The same balance would be preserved were all the world destitute of arms, for all would be alike; but since some will not, others dare not lay them aside.... Horrid mischief would ensue were one half the world deprived of the use of them...."

—*Thomas Paine,*
[one of Founding Fathers of the United States]

And from the world's gentlest human being [the Dalai Lama]:

"If someone has a gun and is trying to kill you, it would be reasonable to shoot back with your own gun."

It is, of course, no coincidence that the right to have guns is one of the earlier freedoms outlined in the United States' Bill of Rights. Without guns in the hands of the people, all the other freedoms are easily negated by the state. If you disagree with that statement, ask yourself if the Nazis could have gassed millions of Jews, had the Jews been armed with rifles and pistols—there weren't enough SS troops to do the job. Lest we forget, in the Warsaw Ghetto Uprising of 1944, a couple of hundred Jews armed with rifles and homemade explosive devices held off two fully equipped German divisions (actually about 8,000 men) for nearly two months.

Closer to home, take the case of the Godhra carnage and the anti-Sikh riots of 1984. Would wanton mobs have slaughtered so many innocent people with such disregard to consequences if their potential victims had been armed and ready to defend themselves? A serious consideration should be given to an armed civilian population as a solution to religious and racial riots as well as other crimes. Since all criminals are instinctively driven by self-preservation, allowing legal ownership of firearms by law-abiding citizens would act as a serious deterrent. This will make sure that if the government fails to

Gun Control and India's Mumbai Massacre

The firearms massacres that have periodically caused shock and horror around the world have been dwarfed by the Mumbai shootings, in which a handful of gunmen left some 500 people killed or wounded.

For anybody who still believed in it, the Mumbai shootings exposed the myth of "gun control". India had some of the strictest firearms laws in the world, going back to the Indian Arms Act, 1878, by which Britain had sought to prevent a recurrence of the Indian mutiny.

Richard Munday,
"Think Tank: If Each of Us Carried a Gun . . . We
Could Combat Terrorism," Sunday Times, December 7, 2008.

do its duty to protect the life and liberty of its citizens (as it has so often done in India's recent past), citizens will be able to protect themselves. . . .

Arguments and Counterarguments

Q1. Won't legal owners of arms use the firearms to kill and murder others? When a man holds a rifle, he becomes almost godlike: Suddenly, he has the ability to deal death and injury to another over a considerable distance—to send, as it were, a thunderbolt of Zeus. For some men, unquestionably, this power is going to be abused, just as some men will always drive a fast car at reckless speeds. For the vast majority of men, however, this power produces precisely the opposite effect: They are humbled by the power they hold, and they become more responsible in its use. That is why, in a nation like the United States with well over 70 million gun owners, only a

49

tiny fraction, less than half a tenth of one percent, use a gun to commit a crime each year. Also since the firearm would be registered with the government along with the owner's address, the type of the firearm, its serial number, etc., those (the criminals) who want to commit crimes will not and DO NOT bother to purchase firearms legally and register them. They can and do buy them from the black market (at a fraction of the cost of a legal firearm, I might add). Legal ownership will allow law-abiding citizens to protect theirs and others' life and property.

Q2. Won't there be a free-for-all during riots? By definition riots ARE free-for-all. However, very few people will participate in riots knowing that a large number of law-abiding citizens own firearms in the area. This will actually prevent riots. Riots are mostly started by miscreants (unscrupulous politicians?) who want to benefit from the chaos of riots. However, the risk (loss of life or limb) for the miscreant in starting and/or participating in such riots, when a large number of the general civilian population owns legal firearms, is significant. Therefore, in most cases, miscreants will not dare to start riots in the first place.

Q3. What about domestic violence and firearms? Domestic violence has nothing to do with firearm ownership. Firearms are merely a tool—not the cause of violence; to quote a famous NRA [National Rifle Association] slogan, "Guns don't kill people, people kill people". Women in India face domestic violence even today with very limited legal gun ownership. If anything, legal firearms in the hands of women might help even the odds—by removing the physical weakness of women from the equation.

Q4. What about accidents? More people in India get killed in automobile accidents than from firearm accidents. In countries where gun ownership rates are high like the United States (which has a firearm to population ratio of approx. 96:100, i.e., almost one firearm for every man, woman and child), Switzerland, New Zealand, etc., several times more people die in road accidents than from firearm accidents. Firearm accidents can be further minimised by making a gun-safety course mandatory before a permit is issued—so long as this is not used as another excuse to delay or deny permits.

Q5. What about firearm-assisted suicides? A suicidal person has many different available ways to end his/her life. Firearms are just another means for him/her. Statistically suicide rates have little correlation with firearm ownership patterns. Many countries with strict anti-gun legislation have high suicide rates and vice versa.

Q6. Are there any working systems and what are the results? Yes, for example in the United States, Switzerland, New Zealand. One must note here that different states in the United States have different degrees of gun ownership and firearm restrictions. Interestingly the states with more restrictions on gun ownerships have a higher crime rate than those that are less restrictive.

People Have the Right to Self-Defense

I do not condone violence or a violent solution to problems, but there can be no justification for not letting people be prepared to defend their own and their families' lives and properties. When one is surrounded by mobs bent on setting him on fire and the like, in a country where policing is nonexistent, owning firearms . . . will have a great deterrent effect on mobs. Of course, if I could sue the police for not giving me complete protection, then I might feel differently (but don't count on it). But by law, the state cannot be at fault for not protecting its citizens. So if the cops take 25 minutes (or several hours) to respond to your call, and in those 25 minutes a criminal kicks open your door, shoots you and your wife, rapes your 11-year-old daughter, and beats your baby to death, that's just tough luck. What about incidents like 1984 and Godhra, where the local administration and police willfully neglected their duty to protect the citizens of this country? . . .

"We live in a country where we have still not cast off the yoke of antiquated laws made by our colonial masters."

Welcome to the Real World

As the Indian law stands today, a citizen of this country cannot even own a stick without inviting a penalty of seven years in prison. We live in a country where we have still not cast off the yoke of antiquated laws made by our colonial masters to keep us oppressed and at the mercy of the government, notwithstanding the lofty vision of the first page of our constitution.

Harping on the few who unfortunately misuse firearms unfairly ignores those millions of us spread all over the world who own and use them responsibly. Dreaming romantically about a world where everything has been made perfectly safe "for the children" is just that, dreaming. I've tried visualising world peace until I'm about ready to have an out of body experience, but as soon as I open my eyes, they're bombing civilians in the northeast or gunning down innocents in Kashmir. Welcome to the real world. [As stated by Patrick Henry, an American revolutionary,]

"I ask, sir, what is the militia? It is the whole people. To disarm the people is the best and most effectual way to enslave them."

Periodical Bibliography

The following articles have been selected to supplement the diverse views presented in this chapter.

Associated Press	"Turks Demand Stricter Gun Control Laws," September 5, 2006. www.gulfnews.com.
Paul Belien	"The French and Their Gun Laws," *Brussels Journal*, December 5, 2007.
Chinascope	"The Party Controls the Gun," September/October 2008.
Haley Sweetland Edwards	"Where Wedding Shots Once Meant Something Else Entirely," Globalpost.com, November 16, 2009. www.globalpost.com.
Michael Friscolanti	"Cops Look at Gun Lock-Ups for Reserves," *Maclean's*, March 9, 2009.
Jonathon Gatehouse, Michael Friscolanti, and Luiza Ch. Savage	"In the Line of Fire," *Maclean's*, April 30, 2007.
Charles Hawley	"A Call for Gun Control in Germany," *Spiegel Online International*, March 16, 2009. www.spiegel.de.
Bruce Laming	"The 1996 Port Arthur Massacre: Implications For Current and Future Cooperative Federalism," *Social Alternatives*, vol. 26, no. 3, 2007.
Peter Lucas	"Disarming Brazil: Lessons and Challenges," *NACLA Report on the Americas*, vol. 41, no. 2, March 1, 2008.
Richard Munday	"Tightening Gun Controls Is Pointless," *Times* (London), March 13, 2009. www.timesonline.co.uk.
Philippine Star	"Briefing on Gun Control," August 18, 2009.

CHAPTER 2

Gun Control and Global Crime

In Nigeria, Mass Gun Ownership Is Not a Solution to Violent Crimes

Okechukwu Emeh Jr.

In the following viewpoint, Nigerian social analyst Okechukwu Emeh Jr. argues mass gun ownership is not the answer to social unrest in Nigeria. Although the country continues to undergo enormous challenges, making guns available to all citizens twenty-one years of age and older will only exacerbate the problems, Emeh says. Instead, he asserts, political leaders and citizens should work together to create a society that values equity and economic progress.

As you read, consider the following questions:

1. As outlined in the viewpoint, what is Jiti Ogunye's main argument?
2. According to the author, why do Scandinavian countries have lower crime rates than Nigeria?
3. Which three African countries exemplify the author's ideals for a successful society?

These are perilous times in Nigeria. The mounting wave of violent crimes in the country has prompted an atmosphere of fear, insecurity, uncertainty and total bewilderment.

Okechukwu Emeh Jr., "Mass Gun Ownership Not a Solution to Violent Crimes in Nigeria," *The Daily Trust*, September 7, 2008, pp. 1–4, Opinion. Reproduced by permission.

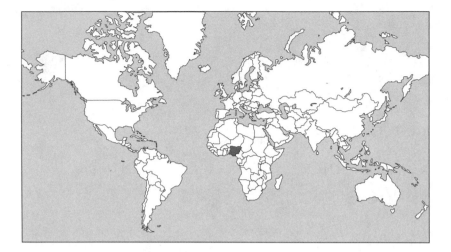

In every nook and cranny of the polity today, the nefarious activities of armed criminals have posed a dangerous threat to hapless Nigerians and impinged on the ability of the Nigerian state to maintain law and order.

Indeed, the ugly situation is so surreal and horrible that one could nurse a déjà vu of a Hobbesian [after the philosopher Thomas Hobbes] state of nature of the premedieval period when life was dull, brutish, nasty and short because of the nihilistic nudging and violence of men. Where do we go from here, as fiendish crimes like armed robbery, assassination, homicide, ritual murder, rape, cultism, kidnapping and gangsterism assume frightening dimension across the length and breadth of the country?

Proposed Solutions

Against the backdrop of the national quandary presented by the upsurge of violent crimes in Nigeria, many concerned Nigerians have been racking their brains on how to wriggle the country out of the severe crisis. One write-up in this direction, which elicited the interest of this writer, a social analyst, was the one published by Mr. Jiti Ogunye in March 2008. In an article, entitled "How to Rescue Nigerians from Armed

Robbery and Firearm Crimes", Ogunye, a legal practitioner, canvassed for a gun ownership policy and legislation that will give every Nigerian above the age of 21 regulated access to mass gun ownership and use. He reasoned that this was necessary and urgent considering a number of factors, including: the constitutional right of every Nigerian to self-defence; the inability of the Nigerian government to guarantee the rights of life, liberty and ownership of property in these times of sharp increase in crime and criminality; nonexistence of crime victims compensation law in the country, which enables family or dependants of crime victims to claim damages in the event of death arising from heinous crimes like armed robbery; the ineptitude of the Nigerian police in securing lives and property of the citizenry; the adverse socioeconomic effects of mass poverty and unemployment and the resultant misery and frustration, which have instigated many Nigerians into armed criminality; and massive circulation of illicit arms that now fan the embers of violent crimes.

"Taking a perspicacious look at the idea, one can see it as a poisoned chalice in the search for a solution to such crimes."

Other factors have also not helped matters in addressing the spiraling wave of violent crimes in Nigeria. These include: years of political misrule, corruption and economic mismanagement and the attendant human deprivation, privation, misery and despondency, which egregiously reached their climax during the immediate past regime of Chief Olusegun Obasanjo; the negation of the ideals of public good by the majority of those in our political helm of affairs; the proliferation of slum neighbourhoods that have become breeding grounds for crime and violence; failure of the Nigerian Prisons Service as a criminal corrective/reformative system; drug abuse and the associated violence; spread of new-generation churches that espouse prosperity gospel that arouses greed and avarice and the precipitate consequences like armed robbery, fraud and prostitution; breakdown of traditional family values through infidelity, incest, divorce, separation, ungodliness, distrust, juvenile delinquency, teenage pregnancy and violence.

Indeed, there is no doubt that the aforementioned factors have aggravated the crisis of violent crimes in Nigeria, a situation that has given impetus to the calls in some quarters for mass gun ownership for self-defence.

However, taking a perspicacious look at the idea, one can see it as a poisoned chalice in the search for a solution to such crimes. For one, a mass gun ownership option could lead to the free flow of illegally acquired arms, which is at the root of the present surge of heinous crimes like armed robbery.

For another, instead of advocating for such a countermeasure, the Nigerian government should be impressed upon to address the underlying factors that have eventuated violent crimes in the country. These particularly include abject poverty, chronic unemployment, social exclusion and the widening gulf between the rich and the poor, as all compounded by the insidious problems of poor governance, economic mismanagement, corruption and shocks of economic reform programmes that have gone awry and failed the generality of Nigerian people.

"Under such world-weary situations, how can one vouch that mass gun ownership would not be a recipe for disaster or mass suicide?"

A Humanistic Response to Crime

Experience from far-flung Western societies shows that they have been able to tame or mollify the morose feelings and frustrations that often ignite the human tendency towards abnormalities like crime and violence. This is achieved through

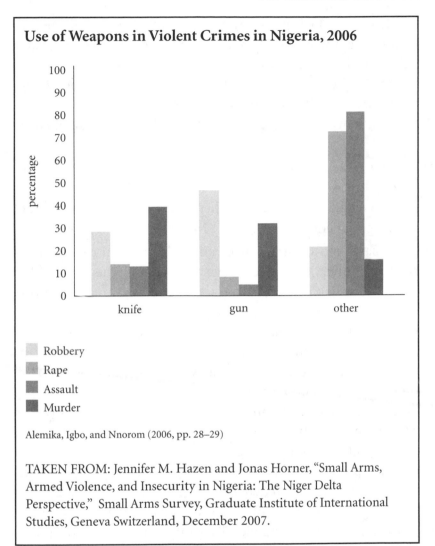

Use of Weapons in Violent Crimes in Nigeria, 2006

- Robbery
- Rape
- Assault
- Murder

Alemika, Igbo, and Nnorom (2006, pp. 28–29)

TAKEN FROM: Jennifer M. Hazen and Jonas Horner, "Small Arms, Armed Violence, and Insecurity in Nigeria: The Niger Delta Perspective," Small Arms Survey, Graduate Institute of International Studies, Geneva Switzerland, December 2007.

a political-economic approach of tackling human depriva-
tions, not through strongman anti-crime measures of increasing the personnel of security agencies and their accoutrement
of law enforcement (including arms and ammunition), extra-
judicial executions and mob justice, as grotesquely often witnessed in Nigeria. For example, in the Scandinavian countries
like the Netherlands, Norway, Sweden, Denmark and Finland,
a pro-Keynesian [after economist John Maynard Keynes] eco-

nomic order, which places high premium on economic growth with development and human welfare through sustained campaigns against unemployment, poverty and social exclusion, has reduced crimes to almost a zero level. This is not to ignore the bold fact that political leaderships there are implacably committed to good governance and liberal policy of social welfare.

The same humanistic response to crime and malignant criminality is re-enacted in African countries that have become symbols of political stability and economic development on the continent like Botswana, Mauritius and Tunisia.

Today, almost nine years of advent of civilian rule in Nigeria, the frontiers of hunger, poverty, unemployment and other forms of human misery are fast expanding and fomenting violent crimes and social unrest across the country. To ask: Under such world-weary situations, how can one vouch that mass gun ownership would not be a recipe for disaster or mass suicide? In truth, adopting such a measure at a fearful time like this would be tantamount to setting a tinderbox of a Bastille [a fortress-prison in France that was overthrown by citizens in 1789] type of social upheaval and mass revolution in the polity. This is not to gloss over the license mass gun ownership could give to violent criminals or psychopathic individuals to unleash mayhem, or the unparallel killings and maiming of lives the policy would generate at the slightest provocation between individuals/groups in times of misunderstanding, especially mindful of the dog-eat-dog nature of our present-day society and considering also the aphorism that a hungry man is an angry man.

Considering the above depressing facts about the dangers of mass gun ownership, what is urgently needed in Nigeria to respond effectively to the skyrocketing rate of violent crimes that are threatening a social Armageddon in the country are structural and institutional approaches. Within the purview of structural approach, this would necessitate the Midas touch of a political economy that would engender a new order where socioeconomic well-being and advancement of Nigerians would be rest-assured by those in our political satrap. This calls for aggressive policy of creation of wealth and job opportunities for our teeming masses—victims of years of deprivation and privation of our successive regimes. This new order to roll back the menace of violent crimes in the polity would also require economic reform programmes that are garbed with a milk of human face. The order also equally demands an affirmation of a new social contract that hums with good governance and general good by political "leaders" at all tiers of government in Nigeria. The new order should be driven by populist and enlightened leadership that would be able to build a just and egalitarian society in a country where everybody will be happy to belong.

Germany's Gun Control Laws Are Ineffective in Preventing Crime

Kevin Yuill

Kevin Yuill teaches American studies at the University of Sunderland, England. In the following viewpoint, he examines the aftermath of the March 11, 2009, German school shooting on conversations about gun control. Citing statistics, Yuill argues that more stringent firearms regulations will not prevent future incidents of gun violence. He also asserts that psychological studies of school shooters have not yielded an identifiable profile. Yuill opposes both attempts at reducing gun violence because, as he contends, they will only further interfere with the lives of law-abiding Germans.

As you read, consider the following questions:

1. According to Yuill, what is the result of the German gun control legislation passed on February 22, 2009?
2. When was the legal age to obtain a gun license in Germany raised to twenty-one?
3. What was the conclusion of the report on school shooters, commissioned by the U.S. Secret Service and the Department of Education?

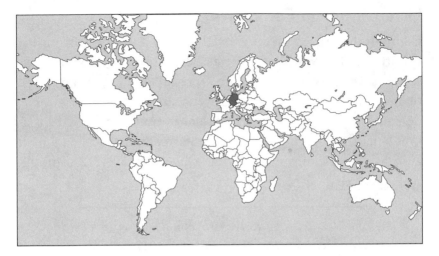

The horrific tragedy in southwest Germany yesterday [March 11, 2009], where 15 people died at the hands of 17-year-old gunman Tim Kretschmer, before he died in a shootout with police, will provoke many questions—especially as it came so soon after a similar shooting spree in Alabama.

The fact that 12 of the dead were pupils and teachers at the Albertville school, at which Kretschmer was a former pupil, added to the horror and the speculation. Murderous rampages like this are thankfully rare. Although that fact will be of little comfort to those who lost loved ones and friends in the melee, this should be the one fact to be remembered when the inevitable question—What might have prevented this devastation?—arises.

Two responses to such a tragedy emerged in the British press and blogosphere. The first, rather knee-jerk, response is to ask why the authorities don't control the estimated 10 million guns possessed by Germans. The second looks to psychological risk profiling in order to spot potential teen killers ahead of time. Yet the Kretschmer shootings demonstrate the pointlessness of both responses.

Increasing Gun Control Measures

Germany has some of the most onerous gun controls of any country in the world, some passed in response to previous school shootings. Ironically, the German parliament approved tighter gun control laws on 22 February this year in a move designed to stop the spread of violent crime. The new legislation bans the carrying of replica firearms and so-called airsoft guns as well as knives with a fixed blade of over 12 centimetres.

"Anyone deemed aggressive, unreliable or with criminal convictions cannot legally buy a gun in Germany."

Previous legislation, passed in April 2008, raised the legal age to obtain a gun licence from 18 to 21. Additional medical and psychological tests were also implemented for under-25s, and pump-action shotguns with pistol-shaped grips were banned. This legislation received a sympathetic hearing after a former pupil injured 11 students at a school in the western town of Emsdetten before turning the gun on himself in 2006. In 2002, a shooting at Gutenberg high school in the town of Erfurt in central Germany came on the day that the country's parliament approved a new bill tightening its already strict gun controls.

People wanting to buy a hunting rifle must undergo background checks that can last up to a year and those wanting a gun for sport must be a member of a club and obtain a licence from police. Anyone deemed aggressive, unreliable or with criminal convictions cannot legally buy a gun in Germany. Gun collectors also need a permit.

A hunter in Saxony spoke this week of the gun control process: 'For hunters and gun club members, they have to answer more than 4,000 questions to get the licence and there is a specific emphasis in teaching and questions on gun law. You have to have everything registered.'

He continued: 'It is pretty strong scrutiny in Germany, but it was ever stricter in GDR (East Germany) times. Not even hunters had their own guns. When we went out hunting, the chief forester handed out the guns and ammunition and every shot was registered and recorded and all guns and ammunition were counted back in at the end of the day.'

The only further precaution that might be taken would be to remove entirely all of the estimated 10 million legally held guns in Germany. However, previous experience should make Germans think twice about the effectiveness of such Draconian measures. Moreover, prohibiting gun ownership would be the equivalent of banning horse riding in the United Kingdom, something that would be regarded as unthinkable. Yet horse riding kills more young girls in Britain than legal firearms kill in Germany. Even if guns were completely banned, anyone with a little bit of time and planning could make a weapon capable of killing many more people.

Psychological Profiling

So this unfortunate incident is a salient demonstration that no law can prevent a shooting spree. But one of the other responses is to try to find some motive in order to be able to prevent future school massacres before they happen. Again, Kretschmer seems to confound the idea that it is possible to predict the possibility of such massacres by psychological profiling.

'There is a preparation time which goes on for weeks and even months', Dr Jens Hoffman, a criminal psychologist at Darmstadt's technical university, told the *Süddeutsche Zeitung* yesterday. Hoffman suggested that a psychological risk-evaluation system could have spotted the killer. It would include questioning to reveal whether a person identified with other teenage killers, had shown off a weapon or had had other problems, including with drugs. Many of the papers noted Kretschmer's targeting of young women and some blog-

Massacres in Countries with Strict Gun Control Laws

Dunblane, Scotland, March 13, 1996

Sana'a, Yemen, March 30, 1997

Taber, Alberta, Canada, April 28, 1999

Veghel, Netherlands, December 7, 1999

Freising, Munich, Germany, February 19, 2002

Erfurt, Thuringia, Germany, April 26, 2002

Vlasenica, Bosnia & Herzegovina, April 29, 2002

The Hague, Netherlands, January 13, 2004

Beslan School, Russia, September 3, 2004

Carmen de Patagones, Buenos Aires Province, Argentina, September 28, 2004

Montreal, Quebec, Canada, September 13, 2006

Paul Valone, "Massacre at Winnenden:
The Failure of German Gun Control,"
Charlotte Gun Rights Examiner, March 13, 2009.

gers wondered whether a type of Asperger's syndrome (presumably the psycho-killer strain of the disease) might be present in mass murderers. In other words, there is an attempt to label this tragedy a result of a disease.

"The lessons drawn from previous incidents about the need for gun controls and personality checks were wrong."

Yet according to press reports, Tim Kretschmer fit none of the existing profiles and appears to have been entirely unremarkable. Studies in the United States have shown the fatuousness of such psychological profiling. There, the Secret Service and the Department of Education commissioned a report into preventing school shootings. After years of careful study, it concluded that: 'There is no accurate or useful "profile" of students who engaged in targeted school violence.' It could only lamely comment that 'many attackers felt bullied, persecuted or injured by others prior to the attack'. That narrows it down, then.

The lesson to be drawn here is that further gun controls would be pointless and that attempts to identify a disease in young men (some press reports spoke of Kretschmer's apparent misogynistic targeting of girls at the school) is wrong-headed. The lessons drawn from previous incidents about the need for gun controls and personality checks were wrong.

The danger remains that intrusion into the lives of ordinary Germans—either in the form of inspecting their homes for guns or the equally odious psychological assessment of young men—might still emerge in the aftermath of this terrible, but extremely unusual event.

Canadian Gun Control Laws Have Reduced Domestic Homicide Rates

Coalition for Gun Control

The Coalition for Gun Control is a Canadian organization formed to reduce gun-related deaths, injuries, and crimes. In the following viewpoint, it argues that stricter gun laws in Canada have proven effective in reducing the number of domestic homicides. Measures, such as licensing gun owners and making extensive background checks on every person who applies for a license, contribute to a lower rate of crimes of passion involving firearms. For this progress to continue, the coalition asserts, Canadians should continue to apply the law and work toward full implementation of it.

As you read, consider the following questions:

1. According to the viewpoint, on average, how many Canadian women killed by their husbands are shot?

2. What are some risk factors for future gun violence that questions on the firearms application form are intended to address, as described in the viewpoint?

3. Between 1974 and 2000, what was the most frequently used weapon in spousal homicides?

Coalition for Gun Control, *Reducing Domestic Homicide*, Coalition for Gun Control, February 5, 2007, pp. 1–3. Reproduced by permission. www.guncontrol.ca.

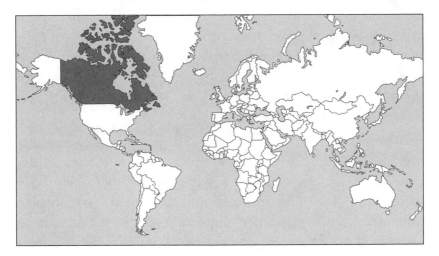

Overview

Throughout the world, guns figure prominently in the cycle of violence against women. Women are at risk of being victimized by their intimate partners. While the vast majority of gun owners are male—and more men are killed with firearms than women—women's experience with firearms is different. Studies of abused women in many corners of the world, including in Canada, report remarkable similarities in the behaviour of abusers, especially amongst those who rely on guns to underpin their violence. Firearms increase the chance that assaults will escalate into murder; are frequently part of the cycle of intimidation and violence that many victims face in their homes; and are used against women when they are present during domestic conflicts. On average, one in three women killed by their husbands in Canada is shot. Often children are also victims, as the presence of firearms not only increases the lethality of domestic violence situations, but the number of victims. For every women killed or injured with a firearm, many more are threatened with guns. A study done in the provinces of New Brunswick and Prince Edward Island on family violence in rural settings found that two-thirds of the women indicated there were firearms in their home said knowing about the firearms made them more fearful for their safety and well-being. Women were more likely to express concern for their safety when the firearms owners were not licensed, and the firearms not registered or safely stored. In Alberta, a shelter worker estimated that at least 40% of her clients had been threatened with a gun.

The presence of firearms is a particular risk factor for domestic homicide. Early studies showed that family and intimate assaults involving firearms were twelve times more likely to result in death than intimate assaults that did not involve firearms. A study of women physically abused by current or former intimate partners in the United States revealed a five-fold increased risk that the abusing partner would murder the woman when he owned a firearm. Recent work reinforces the fact that access to firearms is also one of the top five risk factors associated with domestic murders of women in Canada. In Ontario, a province where only 15% of homes have firearms, 55% of individuals who committed domestic murders of women had access to guns, which reinforces the idea that a gun in the home dramatically increases the risk of death in domestic violence situations.

International research has shown that in industrialized countries, rates of firearm ownership are linked with rates of femicide. Opponents of gun control measures, such as licensing and registration, tend to come from regions where guns are more common, such as rural communities—and in Canada, in the western provinces. However, in these areas firearms figure most prominently in incidents of domestic violence. A study of femicide in 26 developed countries illustrated that there is a strong relationship between the rates of women killed in domestic violence situations and the availability of firearms. These statistics suggest that while violence against women is endemic, rates of death are higher in contexts where guns are prevalent, as guns increase the lethality or risk of death in those violent situations.

The Role of the Law

The role of firearms legislation in protecting women has been well [supported]. The United Nations Commission on Crime Prevention and Criminal Justice maintained that strong controls on firearms were needed to protect women from violence and in 1997 explicitly recognized the need to strengthen regulations on firearms in order to address violence against women. The resolution outlined the key elements of effective legislation, including licensing, registration and safe storage. Licensing is intended to reduce the chance that those who present a risk for violent action have access to firearms. Registration is intended to help enforce licensing and to reduce the chances that legal guns will be diverted into illegal markets. Safe storage also reduces the risk that these guns will be used impulsively. These measures are in place in most countries worldwide, although combating violence against women is still not always a priority.

In Canada, the murder of 14 young women at an engineering school on December 6, 1989, by a man who shouted "you are all a bunch of feminists," focused attention on the role of firearms in violence against women. As well, several high-profile inquiries into domestic violence cases drew attention and stressed the importance of licensing gun owners and registering firearms. Legislation which was developed in 1991 (Bill C-17) and then strengthened in 1995 (Bill C-68, the Firearms Act), explicitly included provisions aimed at reducing access to guns amongst those with a history of violence against women. While the screening process was strengthened in 1991, it was further improved in 1995. Licensing gun owners is an essential measure to keep guns away from potentially abusive spouses, and individuals with a history of violence. A substantial proportion of men who kill their partners have either criminal records or a history of psychiatric treatment. In many of these cases, other members of the community have known that these threats and acts of violence were occurring. Under the law, extensive background checks are conducted on every person who applies for a license. The questions on the firearms application form are directly linked to studies of domestic homicides and suicide involving firearms. A number of risk factors were identified in those studies: a history of violence, past substance abuse (drugs and alcohol), an existing criminal record, a separation or pending separation, depression, or employment and financial problems. The 1995 legislation requires current and former spouses (from the past two years) to be notified when an applicant applies for a firearms license, and continuous monitoring of firearm licensees is intended to ensure that license eligibility is immediately reviewed when there is a domestic violence incident. A toll-free line was created for spouses of applicants or others who may have concerns about their safety. There have been 22,523 firearm licenses refused or revoked between 1999 and 2008 because the individual in question was deemed a potential risk to themselves or to others.

"In Canada, homicides of women with firearms dropped by over 63 percent with progressive strengthening of gun laws (1991–2005)."

While some argue that owning guns is a right, international experts maintain that governments have an obligation to regulate firearms in order to reduce the risks of violence. The UN Special Rapporteur on Violence Against Women and the Special Rapporteur on Small Arms and Human Rights emphasized that states which do not adequately regulate firearms are failing to meet their obligations under international law.

Women Are Safer Because of Stronger Gun Laws

To date there is considerable evidence that strengthening firearm legislation is often of particular benefit to women: In

Australia, the United Kingdom and Canada, stronger firearm laws were accompanied by greater decreases in murders of women than in male homicide. Canada's gun law is used by police to remove guns from dangerous people and to investigate crimes. The online licensing and registration system also provides police with round-the-clock access to information about the presence of legal firearms when they answer domestic violence calls. In 2009, police officers across Canada consulted the gun registry 10,800 times a day. In Canada, homicides of women with firearms dropped by over 63 percent with progressive strengthening of gun laws (1991–2005), while murders of women with other means (stabbing, beating, etc.) declined by only 38 percent. Firearms were the most frequently used weapon in the commission of spousal homicides between 1974 and 2000, accounting for the death of one in three victims. The latest statistical report published on family violence in Canada has demonstrated that significant decreases have occurred in the use of firearms in spousal and other intimate partner homicides. Since the introduction of the Firearms Act, the rate of firearm-related spousal homicide decreased by two-thirds, from 1.7 per million spouses in 1996 to 0.5 per million spouses in 2007. While firearms were used in approximately 40 percent of murders of women in 1989, they now account for under 15 percent, in part due to stricter controls on firearms.

Conclusion

Gun control is not a panacea, but it is intended to reduce the risk that those who present a threat to themselves or others will have access to firearms. Specific measures were considered, when developing Canada's 1995 Firearms Act, to address the particular role of legally owned firearms in the murder, injury and intimidation of women and children in the home. Although the law has not been fully implemented, there is evidence that it is working and has prevented tragedies. Reducing the threat of firearms in domestic violence requires implementation in the community as well as an integrated approach.

Australia's Gun Control Policies Have Reduced Crime

Simon Chapman, Philip Alpers, Kingsley Agho, and Mike Jones

Simon Chapman, Philip Alpers, Kingsley Agho, and Mike Jones are professors in the Sydney School of Public Health at the University of Sydney in New South Wales, Australia. In the following viewpoint, the authors argue that following the passage of stricter gun laws in Australia in 1996, rates of firearm-related deaths, suicides, and mass killings have plummeted. They credit the gun buyback program and other legislative reforms for taking guns off the streets and out of the hands of would-be murderers.

As you read, consider the following questions:

1. How many guns were purchased by the Australian federal government during the 1996–97 firearms buyback program?

2. What percentage of firearms deaths per year are attributed to suicides?

3. What was the average increase in unintentional firearms deaths between 1996 and 2003?

Abstract

Background: After a 1996 firearm massacre in Tasmania in which 35 people died, Australian governments united to re-

Simon Chapman, Philip Alpers, Kingsley Agho, and Mike Jones, "Australia's 1996 Gun Law Reforms: Faster Falls in Firearm Deaths, Firearm Suicides, and a Decade Without Mass Shootings," *Injury Prevention*, vol. 12, December 2006, pp. 365–366, 368, 370–371. Copyright © 2006 British Medical Association. Reproduced by permission.

move semi-automatic and pump-action shotguns and rifles from civilian possession, as a key component of gun law reforms.

Objective: To determine whether Australia's 1996 major gun law reforms were associated with changes in rates of mass firearm homicides, total firearm deaths, firearm homicides and firearm suicides, and whether there were any apparent method substitution effects for total homicides and suicides.

Design: Observational study using official statistics. Negative binomial regression analysis of changes in firearm death rates and comparison of trends in pre–post gun law reform firearm-related mass killings.

Setting: Australia, 1979–2003.

Main outcome measures: Changes in trends of total firearm death rates, mass fatal shooting incidents, rates of firearm homicide, suicide and unintentional firearm deaths, and of total homicides and suicides per 100,000 population.

Results: In the 18 years before the gun law reforms, there were 13 mass shootings in Australia, and none in the 10.5 years afterwards. Declines in firearm-related deaths before the law reforms accelerated after the reforms for total firearm deaths (p = 0.04), firearm suicides (p = 0.007) and firearm homicides (p = 0.15), but not for the smallest category of unintentional firearm deaths, which increased. No evidence of substitution effect for suicides or homicides was observed. The rates per 100,000 of total firearm deaths, firearm homicides and firearm suicides all at least doubled their existing rates of decline after the revised gun laws.

Conclusions: Australia's 1996 gun law reforms were followed by more than a decade free of fatal mass shootings, and accelerated declines in firearm deaths, particularly suicides. Total homicide rates followed the same pattern. Removing large numbers of rapid-firing firearms from civilians may be an effective way of reducing mass shootings, firearm homicides and firearm suicides.

On 10 May 1996, 12 days after 35 people were shot dead and 18 seriously wounded by a gunman at Port Arthur, Tasmania, Australia's state and federal governments agreed to enact uniform gun control laws. Between June 1996 and August 1998, the new restrictions were progressively implemented in all six states and two territories. As the Port Arthur gunman and several other mass killers had used semi-automatic weapons, the new gun laws banned rapid-fire long guns, specifically to reduce their availability for mass shootings. Under the 1996–7 Australian Firearms Buyback, 643,726 newly prohibited semi-automatic and pump-action rifles and shotguns were purchased by the federal government from their civilian owners at market value, funded by a levy on income tax.[1] Tens of thousands of gun owners also voluntarily surrendered additional, non-prohibited firearms without compensation.[2] In total, more than 700,000 guns were removed and destroyed from an adult population of about 12 million. Australia's revised gun laws also require that all firearms be individually registered to their licensed owners, that private firearm sales be prohibited and that each gun transfer through a licensed arms dealer be approved only after the police are satisfied of a genuine reason for ownership. In this context, possession of or self-defence in Australia is specifically prohibited civilians are licensed to possess handguns. A detailed ...ary of the reforms can be found in Ozanne-Smith *et al.*[3]

In Australian federal law, firearm means "a device designed or adapted to discharge shot, bullets, or other projectiles by means of an explosive charge or a compressed gas".[4] Legislation in all Australian states and territories echoes this definition, and all include airguns and compressed gas guns in their definition of a firearm.[5]

Using publicly available data, we examined Australian firearm death rates before and after the Port Arthur massacre and the gun law reforms it precipitated to explore the hypothesis that the introduction of the gun laws was associated with an accelerating decline in deaths caused by firearms. We also examine all-cause homicides and all-method suicides in order to assess the possibility that substitution effects may have occurred: that reduced access to firearms may have caused those with homicidal or suicidal intent to use substitute methods.

"More than 700,000 guns were removed and destroyed from an adult population of about 12 million."

Methods

Data on unintentional (accidental), and intentional (suicide and homicide) deaths caused by firearms were obtained from the National Injury Surveillance Unit,[6i] sourced from the Australian Bureau of Statistics (ABS) mortality data collection 1979–2003, coded as International Classification of Diseases, 9th revision and 10th revision. This represents a census of all firearm deaths in Australia for those 25 years. In all Australian jurisdictions (state and territory Firearms Acts and Regula-

i These figures were updated in a private correspondence from NISU on 16 October 2006 (table 2 [not shown]).

Abbreviation ABS, Australian Bureau of Statistics

tions), at federal level (the Customs Act and Regulations) and in the ABS mortality collection, "firearm" includes guns whose projectiles are propelled by compressed air or gas. Although we know of no such fatalities, any deaths from airguns or ball bearing guns would be included in this dataset.

Population data were obtained from the ABS for the same period. Firearm death rates per 100,000 were then calculated. The trend in these rates for the 18 years up to and including the year in which the new firearm laws were announced (1996) were compared with the corresponding trend for the next 7 years (1997–2003), to examine the hypothesis that the announcement and implementation of the gun laws were associated with an acceleration in the existing decline in firearm homicides, firearm suicides and total firearm deaths. Fatal "legal intervention" shootings by police, which averaged 4.5 per annum, were excluded as they were not targeted by the gun laws in question. For the post–Port Arthur period, rates of total all-cause (and non-gun) homicides and suicides were also examined, to consider whether perpetrators may have substituted other means of killing if the gun laws reduced their access to firearms.

Numbers of deaths by category (total and components) have been viewed as arising from an overdispersed Poisson process and analyzed using negative binomial regression, with annual Australian population estimates used as an offset. In practical terms, the model views deaths as a number of events per head of population, although for convenience we report rates per 100,000 heads of population. The model has been used to estimate the change in trend of the relative rate of firearm deaths associated with the introduction of uniform gun laws. Given that the rate of firearm deaths had been decreasing before the harmonization of gun laws, the statistical question addressed is not just whether death rates were lower after the laws were changed, as the pre-existing trend would predict this even in the absence of changed laws, but whether the rate of decrease in firearm deaths seems to be greater after the gun laws were announced. Given the observational nature of the data available, we can directly comment on the association of gun law harmonization and firearm-related death rates, but conclusions regarding causality of the association must remain interpretive rather than definitive. However, as it would be politically almost inconceivable that any government would conduct a randomized controlled trial of gun law effects, the evidence presented must be among the best that could ever be available to deal with the question of the effects of such law reform. As counts are of deaths, it is reasonable to assume that observations are independent across years. Three models have been fitted for each type of firearm death.

$$\ln \{deaths/population\} = \beta_{00} + \beta_{10} \times year, year = 1979, \ldots, 1996$$

(a)

$$\ln \{deaths/population\} = \beta_{01} + \beta_{11} \times year, year = 1997, \ldots, 2003$$

(b)

$$\ln \{deaths/population\} = \beta_{02} + \beta_{12} \times year + \beta_{22} Law_j + \beta_{32} \times year \times Law_j, year = 1979, \ldots, 2003, j = 0,1 \quad (c)$$

Models (a) and (b) are used to estimate the trend (measured as average annual change in rate/100,000 population) in gun deaths before and after the introduction of gun laws, through the terms $e^{\beta 10}$ and $e^{\beta 11}$ respectively. Model (c) is used to estimate the effect on trends in firearm-related deaths associated with the introduction of gun laws through the interaction term "year×law". As the model is parameterized, $\beta_{32} = \beta_{11} - \beta_{10}$ and therefore $e^{\beta 32}$ estimates the ratio of trend after introduction to that before the introduction of the gun laws. Trends and relative trends have been reported as relative rates (before and after 1996) and relative trends (comparing periods) with 95% confidence intervals. The statistical significance of the relative trends has also been reported. Analysis has been undertaken separately in firearm-related and non-firearm-related deaths as well as total deaths for homicide and suicide to investigate possible substitution effects. If substitution occurred, we would expect an increasing downward trend in firearm deaths after the introduction of gun control laws but a compensatory lesser downward or even upward trend in non-firearm-related deaths over the same period. The extent of influence of mass shootings has been investigated by repeating firearm-related homicides excluding mass (≥ 5 victims died) shootings.

An alternate view of these data might have been as a time series of mortality rates, as was done by gun lobby affiliated researchers Baker and McPhedran.[7] However, we saw two disadvantages to this approach. One is that calculating mortality rates and then treating them as a number in a time series ignores the natural variability inherent in the counts that make up the numerator of the rate. Another is that the Box–Jenkins class of models, including the auto-regressive integrated moving average model used by Baker and McPhedran,[7] is unable to explicitly address the effect of an intervention such as the introduction of gun laws. Interpretation of these models is reduced to comparing the mortality rates expected under a model assuming no effect of the intervention with that observed, both in the post-intervention period. This is however an insensitive approach, and its interpretation is not based on formal statistical inference but rather on visual inspection and qualitative interpretation of graphs, which may be prone to selectivity.

The second author has archived reports of all mass shooting incidents in Australia (defined here as when ≥ 5 victims died; table 1). These were used to compare the incidence of such shootings before and after the introduction of the new gun laws.

Results

In the 18 years up to and including 1996, the year of the massacre at Port Arthur, Australia experienced 13 mass shootings. In these events alone, 112 people were shot dead and at least another 52 wounded (table 1).[8] In the 10.5 years since Port Arthur and the revised gun laws, no mass shootings have occurred in Australia. Figure 1 [not shown] comprises seven graphs plotting both pre-law and post-law data and trends for (a) firearm homicide death rate, (b) non-firearm homicide death rate, (c) firearm homicide minus mass shootings death rate, (d) unintentional firearm death rate, (e) firearm suicide death rate, (f) non-firearm suicide death rate and (g) total firearm death rate.

Each graph presents the observed annual death rate (triangles) and the expected death rate under the hypothesis of an effect of gun laws (dots) estimated from a negative binomial model. The vertical line on the horizontal axis indicates the revision of gun laws commencing in 1996.

An interpretive note that applies to all the graphs in fig 1 [not shown] is that the shape of fitted lines (trend pre-law and trend post-law) involves two components. The first is that the post-law trend line is shifted upward or downward according to the underlying rates of mortality in the pre-gun law and post-gun law periods. Where there is a pre-existing downward trend in mortality, such a shift would occur regardless of the effect of gun laws. The more interesting component is how much the slopes of the pre-gun law and post-gun law trends differ. Although it can be difficult to judge the magnitude from the graph itself, this is quantified in the final column of table 3 [not shown], which provides estimates of the relative slopes of the post- to pre-law trends.

Total firearm deaths. Table 2 [not shown] shows that gun-related deaths (both in numbers and as a rate per 100,000) had been steadily falling throughout the years before the new gun laws were announced. In the 18 years (1979–96), there were 11,299 firearm deaths (annual average 627.7). In the 7 years for which reliable data are available after the announcement of the new gun laws, there were 2,328 firearm deaths, (annual average 332.6). Figure 1G and table 3 [not shown] indicate that although the rate per 100,000 of total firearm deaths was reducing by an average of 3% per year, this rate doubled to 6% after the introduction of gun laws. The ratio of trend estimates differed statistically from 1 (no effect; p = 0.03). The decline in total firearm deaths thus accelerated after the introduction of the gun laws.

Firearm suicides. Firearm suicides represent the largest component cause of total firearm deaths in Australia (more than three in four of all firearm deaths). In the 18 years (1979–96), there were 8850 firearm suicides (annual average 491.7). In the 7 years for which reliable data are available after the announcement of the new gun laws, there were 1726 firearm suicides, an annual average of 246.6. Figure 1E and table 3 [not shown] indicate that while the rate of firearm suicide was reducing by an average of 3% per year, this more than doubled to 7.4% per year after the introduction of gun laws. The ratio of trend estimates differed statistically from 1 (no effect; p = 0.007). Again, we conclude that the decline in total firearm suicides accelerated after the introduction of the gun laws.

Firearm homicides. In the 18 years (1979–96), there were 1672 firearm homicides (annual average 92.9). In the 7 years for which reliable data are available after the announcement of the new gun laws, there were 389 firearm homicides, an annual average of 55.6. Figure 1A and table 3 [not shown] show that while the rate of firearm homicide was reducing by an average of 3% per year, this increased to 7.5% per year after the introduction of gun laws. However, the ratio of trend estimates failed to reach statistical significance (p = 0.15) because of the low power inherent in the small numbers involved.

Table 1: Mass Shootings * in Australia, January 1979–October 2006

Date	Location and State	Victims Killed by Gunshot	Perpetrators Killed	Total Killed by Gunshot	Victims Wounded	Perpetrators
28 April 1996	Port Arthur, TAS	35	0	35	19	Martin Bryant
25 January 1996	Hillcrest, QLD	6	1	7	0	Peter May
31 March 1993	Cangai, NSW	5	1	6	0	Leabeater and Steele
27 October 1992	Terrigal, NSW	6	0	6	1	Malcolm Baker
17 August 1991	Strathfield, NSW	6	1	7	7	Wade Frankum
30 August 1990	Surry Hills, NSW	5	0	5	0	Paul Evers
25 September 1988	Oenpelli, NT	6	0	6	0	Dennis Rostron
8 December 1987	Queen St, VIC	8	1	9	5	Frank Vitkovic
10 October 1987	Canley Vale, NSW	5	1	6	1	John Tran
9 August 1987	Hoddle St, VIC	7	0	7	19	Julian Knight
19 June 1987	Top End, NT/WA	5	1	6	0	Josef Schwab
1 June 1984	Wahroonga, NSW	5	1	6	0	John Brandon
24 September 1981	Campsie, NSW	5	1	6	0	Fouad Daoud
Total		104	8	112	52	

*Definitions of "mass shooting" and "mass homicide" have ranged from 3 to 5 victims killed. To exclude most of the more common firearm-related spousal and family violence killings, "mass shooting" is defined here as one in which ≥5 firearm-related homicides are committed by one or two perpetrators in proximate events in a civilian setting, not counting any perpetrators killed by their own hand or otherwise. Details of each case were collected from police and coroners' files, by personal communication with police and counsel involved, or as a last resort from corroborating newspaper reports.

TAKEN FROM: Simon Chapman, Philip Alpers, Kingsley Agho, and Mike Jones, "Australia's 1996 Gun Law Reforms: Faster Falls in Firearm Deaths, Firearm Suicides, and a Decade Without Mass Shootings," *Injury Prevention*, December 2006.

When all firearm mass homicides (≥5 victims shot dead per incident) were removed from the data (fig 1C and table 3 [not shown]), the conclusions were only slightly altered. The reason for this slight change is that all mass shootings in Australia in the years studied occurred before the introduction of gun laws (table 1). This increases the apparent downward trend in the pre-gun law period (0.971 when all homicides are considered, v 0.961 when mass shootings are removed, table 3 [not shown]). The trend in the post-gun law period is unaffected.

Unintentional firearm deaths. Unintentional (accidental) firearm deaths have always been the smallest component of the total firearm deaths in Australia, representing around 6% of all firearm deaths. Figure 1D and table 2 [not shown] indicate that although the rate of total gun deaths reduced by an average of 7.6% per year, the rate of unintentional gun deaths actually increased by 8.5% per year after the introduction of the gun laws. We discuss this finding below.

Total homicides. Figure 1B and table 3 [not shown] indicate that the rate of total non-firearm homicides increased by an average of 1.1% per year before the introduction of the gun law and reduced by an average of 2.4% per year after the introduction of the gun laws (see row 3, columns 2 and 3, respectively, in table 3 [not shown]). The ratio of the pre-law to post-law trends differ to a significant extent (p = 0.05).

Table 2 [not shown] also shows the total homicides (by all methods) for the period 1979–2003. In the pre-gun law period, total non-firearm homicides were essentially stable and did not differ from steady state to a statistically significant extent (table 3 [not shown]). After the introduction of gun laws, a significant downward trend was evident in total homicides, and the ratio of pre-law to post-law trends differed statistically from "no effect" (p = 0.01, table 3 [not shown]). We conclude that the data do not support any homicide method substitution hypothesis.

Total suicides. Figure 1F and table 3 [not shown] indicate that the rate of total non-firearm suicides increased by an average of 2.3% per year before the introduction of the gun law and reduced by an average of 4.1% per year after the introduction of the gun laws (see row 6, columns 2 and 3, respectively in table 3 [not shown]). The ratio of the pre-law to-post-law trends differs statistically (p<0.001).

Table 2 [not shown] also shows total suicides for the period under review. Total suicides follow a similar pattern as total non-firearm homicides. In the pre-gun law period, total suicides were essentially stable (table 3 [not shown]). After the introduction of gun laws a significant downward trend was evident in total suicides and the ratio of pre-law to post-law trends differs statistically from "no effect" (p<0.001; table 3 [not shown]). We conclude that the data do not support any suicide method substitution hypothesis.

In all, total suicide (all methods including firearms) increased by an average of 1% per year before the introduction of the gun laws and decreased by an average of 4.4% per year after the introduction of the gun laws, whereas, total homicide (all methods including firearms) was essentially steady (decreasing by an average of 0.1% per year) before the introduction of the gun law and decreased further by 3.3% per year after the introduction of the gun law. The ratio of the pre-law to post-law trends reaches statistical significance for both total suicide (p<0.001) and total homicide (p = 0.01; table 3 [not shown]).

Discussion

After 11 mass shootings in a decade and 13 in the 18 years before the introduction of the new gun control laws, Australia collected and destroyed categories of firearms designed to kill many people quickly. In his immediate reaction to the Port Arthur massacre, Australian Prime Minister John Howard said of semi-automatic long guns: "There is no legitimate interest served in my view by the free availability in this country of weapons of this kind. . . Every effort should be made to ensure such an incident does not occur again. That is why we have proposed a comprehensive package of reforms designed to implement tougher, more effective and uniform gun laws."[9],[10]

In the 10.5 years which followed the gun buyback announcement (May 1996–October 2006), no mass shootings have occurred in Australia. As one study on the Australian firearm buyback notes: "Given that mass murders cause so much community fear, it is appropriate to choose this as an evaluation outcome separate from homicide rates generally."[11] Yet, in a recent paper examining the same dataset,[7] two authors with declared affiliations with firearm advocacy groups failed entirely to report on this fundamental outcome, and issued press releases headlined *Gun Laws Failed to Improve Safety* and *New Research Vindicates Gun Owners*.[12],[13] Given that the banning of semi-automatic rifles and pump-action shotguns was premised on the explicit objective of reducing the likelihood of mass shootings, such a flagrant omission from their analysis is extraordinary.

"'There is no legitimate interest served in my view by the free availability in this country of weapons of this kind.'"

We suggest an analogy here. If a government addressed a recurrent incidence of level crossing car/train collisions by mandating alarmed barrier gates, it would be appropriate to ask two questions when later evaluating the effect of such a measure. One could ask "Have there been fewer level crossing car/train collisions and fatalities?" and "Have there been fewer road toll deaths from any cause?" The outlawing of rapid-fire rifles and shotguns in the revised Australian gun laws was the equivalent of level crossing barrier gate legislation: its primary intention was to reduce mass shootings, a national concern after the Port Arthur massacre. Accelerating the reduction in overall firearm deaths—as occurred—is a bonus, particularly as the data show that there is no evidence of method substitution for either suicide or homicide.

Three categories dominate firearm death data in Australia: suicide, homicide and unintentional (accidental) shootings. Suicide is the leading category, with an average of 79% of all firearm deaths each year. Firearms have a high lethality index (or "completion rate") in both homicide and suicide.[14] Had the gun law reforms not occurred, more Australians contemplating suicide—in particular, impulsive young people—might have more easily found a method of instant completion. Reliable national data on suicide attempts are not available in Australia to examine whether suicide completion rates changed after Port Arthur. However, the data show that the declining rate of suicide by firearms accelerated significantly after the 1996 gun laws, with there being no apparent substitution by other methods.

As only a single shot is involved in most firearm suicides, it might be argued that reduced access to rapid-firing semi-automatic weapons would be irrelevant in policies designed to reduce suicide: a person intending suicide with a firearm need use only a single-shot gun. However, a person attempting suicide might just as easily use any available gun, including one capable of firing rapidly. The removal of more than 700,000 guns from an adult population of around 12 million therefore may have reduced access to guns among potential suicide attempters.

> *"Had the gun law reforms not occurred, more Australians contemplating suicide . . . might have more easily found a method of instant completion."*

However, many gun owners own >1 firearm and may well have handed in the newly prohibited weapons after the new laws required this, but retained their non-prohibited weapons. This means that although 700,000 firearms were removed from the community, the number of persons (and households) with access to (still legal) firearms is unlikely to have reduced significantly. What can be said with certainty though is that 700,000 fewer guns were available to be stolen or otherwise leaked from lawful owners to criminals.

The finding that there was a significant increase in unintentional (accidental) firearm deaths after the new gun laws is perplexing, although it should be emphasized that the numbers involved in this increase are small. The average annual increase in unintentional firearm deaths in the 7 years since 1996 was just 1.4 deaths. We can conceive of no plausible hypothesis as to why the removal of more than 700,000 guns from the population, the introduction of firearm registration and the tightening of shooter licensing procedures would be associated with an increase in unintentional fatal shootings, however small in number.

There are considerable problems in accurately estimating the number of gun owners and guns in a community. Given the political volatility of gun control, and the widespread and virulent opposition of many firearm owners to gun laws, which is often manifested in statements of open defiance on gun lobby Web sites and publications, under-reporting of gun ownership is common in both survey research and in police registers of licensed gun owners. In 1992, Kellerman *et al* reported that owners of registered handguns were much more likely to be prepared to answer questions about gun ownership than about their income.[15] However, licensed firearm owners are those who self-select to obey shooter licensing requirements. Before the 1996 gun law reforms, there was no national system of firearm registration in Australia, so there is no way of accurately comparing the estimated number of guns in the Australian community before the 1996 gun laws with the known number of registered guns after the introduction of the laws. Notwithstanding these uncertainties, in a trend that preceded the Australian Firearms Buyback but seems to have been greatly accelerated by it, the reported private gun ownership fell by 45% between 1989 and 2000, leaving a three times less likelihood of an Australian household reporting owning a firearm compared with a US household.[16] By destroying an estimated one- fifth of their country's estimated stock of firearms—the equivalent figure in the US would be 40 million guns[17]—Australians have chosen to significantly shrink their private arsenal. All remaining guns must now be individually registered to their licensed owners, private (owner-to-owner) firearm sales are no longer permitted, and each gun purchase through a licensed arms dealer is scrutinized by the police to establish a "genuine reason" for ownership. Possession of firearms for self-defence is specifically prohibited, and very few civilians are permitted to own handguns. Australia's state governments, police forces and police unions all supported the tightened gun laws. In 2002–3, Australia's rate of 0.27 firearm-related homicides per 100,000 population was one-fifteenth that of the US.[18,19]

It would also be negligent to omit what seemed plain to Australians, but could be less easy to measure in empirical terms. After the death and serious injury of 54 people at Port Arthur, facilitated by firearms then openly marketed by licensed gun dealers as "assault weapons", a national upwelling of grief and revulsion saw pollsters reporting 90–95% public approval for stringent new gun laws.[20,21] Resistance to gun control was roundly condemned in virtually all news media,[22] and governments' 12 days of resolve deprived the firearm lobby of crucial delay time. Announcing the law changes, Prime Minister John Howard invoked the majority will of Australians when he said "This represents an enormous shift in the culture of this country towards the possession, the use and the ownership of guns. It is a historic agreement. It means that this country, through its governments, has decided not to go down the American path ... Ours is not a gun culture, ours is a culture of peaceful cooperation."[23],[24] Later opinion polling ranked Howard's new gun laws as by far the most popular decision in the first year of his conservative government.[25] In the opinion of the authors, the 1996 sea change in Australian attitudes—and perhaps also a significant component of the public health benefits of lower rates of firearm-related mass shootings, suicide and homicide reported here—is best described as a national change of attitude to gun owners and their firearms.

Limitations. Table 2 [not shown] shows that across the 25 years, there were 200 firearm deaths classified as being of undetermined intent. Of these, 157 (80.1%) occurred before 1991, and only 15–23 after 1996. (To preserve victims' privacy, publicly released data for years in which there are ≥3 firearm deaths of undetermined intent are recorded as NA. This was the case for 4 of 7 years between 1997 and 2003, meaning that there could have been a maximum of 12 and a minimum of 4 undetermined cases in this time.) Across the study period, firearm deaths of unknown intent comprised 1.3% of all firearm deaths, falling to 0.8% after 1990 and 0.4% after 1996. The decrease in "unknowns" is attributed to improved reporting practices. These "missing data" from the component analyses of firearm suicide, homicides and unintentional deaths may account for small variations in the results shown, were their status able to be known.

Although ABS mortality data were also available for 2004, the National Injury Surveillance Unit warned of significant questions of accuracy due to the number of coroners' cases not closed at the time, and potential miscoding of suicide, homicide and unintentional firearm-related death in that year.[26] Accordingly, this study ends with 2003, the most recent year of reliable data.

Implications for prevention. The data swings shown are so obvious that if one were given the data in table 2 [not shown] and were asked to guess the date of a major firearm intervention, it would be clear that it happened between 1996 and 1998. The Australian Firearms Buyback remains the world's most sweeping gun collection and destruction program.[27] A combination of laws making semi-automatic and pump-action shotguns and rifles illegal, paying market price for surrendered weapons, and registering the remainder were the central ingredients. The Australian example provides evidence that removing large numbers of firearms from a community can be associated with a sudden and ongoing decline in mass shootings and accelerating declines in total firearm-related deaths, firearm homicides and firearm suicides.

"The Australian Firearms Buyback remains the world's most sweeping gun collection and destruction program."

Key points

- A radical gun law reform occurred in Australia after a gun massacre (35 dead and 18 seriously injured) in April 1996. Semi-automatic and pump-action shotguns and rifles were banned; a tax-funded firearm buyback and amnesties saw over 700,000 guns surrendered from an adult population of about 12 million.

- The total firearm deaths, firearm homicides and firearm suicides had been falling in the 18 years preceding the new gun laws. In all, 13 mass shootings were noticed in the 18 years preceding the new gun laws.

- In the 10.5 years after the gun law reforms, there have been no mass shootings, but accelerated declines in annual total gun deaths and firearm suicides and a non-significant accelerated decline in firearm homicides. No substitution effects occurred for suicides or homicides.

Acknowledgements

We thank Renate Kriesfeld, National Injury Surveillance Unit, South Australia, for providing data. We also thank our three reviewers for their extremely helpful reviews.

Authors' affiliations. S Chapman, P Algers, K Agho, M Jones, School of Public Health, University of Sydney, New South Wales, Australia.

Competing interests: SC was a member of the Coalition for Gun Control (Australia) from 1993 to 1996. PA is the editor of Gun Policy News (www.gunpolicy.org/). All authors had full access to all of the data in the study and MJ and KA take responsibility for the integrity of the data and the accuracy of the data analysis.

References

1. **Commonwealth Attorney-General's Department, Australia**. *The Australian Firearms Buyback: tally for number of firearms collected and compensation paid.* Canberra: CAGD, 2002.

2. **Giles T**. Amnesty tally 40,000 guns. *Herald-Sun*. Melbourne, 22 April, 2002.

3. **Ozanne-Smith J**, Ashby K, Newstead S, *et al.* Firearm related deaths: the impact of regulatory reform. *Inj Prev* 2004;10:280–6.

4. **Customs (Prohibited Imports) Regulations 1998; Regulation 4F**. In force under the Customs Act, 1901.

5. **Alpers P**, Twyford C. *Small arms in the Pacific.* Occasional Paper No 8. Geneva: Small Arms Survey, 2003, 74–80. http://www.smallarmssurvey.org/files/sas/publications/o_papers.html (accessed 13 Nov 2006).

6. **Kreisfeld R**. Firearm deaths and hospitalisations in Australia. NISU Briefing. Adelaide: National Injury Surveil-

lance Institute, Australian Institute of Health and Welfare, 2005, 2. http://www.nisu.flinders.edu.au/briefs/firearm_deaths_2005.pdf (accessed 13 Nov 2006).

7. **Baker J**, McPhedran S. Gun laws and sudden death. Did the Australian firearms legislation of 1996 make a difference? *Br J Criminol* 2006. Advance access 18 Oct. doi: 10.1093/bjc/921084.

8. **Alpers P**. *Mass gun killers: ten-year survey challenges myths. Mental Health Quarterly.* Wellington: New Zealand Mental Health Foundation, 1996:22–3.

9. **Denholm M**. Howard vow on gun law massacre in Tasmania. *Daily Telegraph.* Sydney, 30 Apr, 1996.

10. **Howard J**. Never, ever again. Prime Ministerial Op-ed. *Herald Sun.* Melbourne, 10 May, 1996.

11. **Reuter P**, Mouzos J. Australia: A massive buyback of low-risk guns. In: Ludwig J, Cook P, eds. *Evaluating gun policy: effects on crime and violence.* Washington, DC: Brookings Institute, 2003:141.

12. **McPhedran S**. *Study: gun laws failed to improve safety,* Media release. Ballarat: International Coalition for Women in Shooting and Hunting (WiSH), 2006.

13. **Baker J**. *New Research Vindicates Gun Owners,* Media release. Adelaide: Sporting Shooters Association of Australia (SA) Inc, 2006.

14. **Beaman V**, Annest JL, Mercy JA, *et al.* Lethality of firearm-related injuries in the United States population. *Ann Emerg Med* 2000;35:258–66.

15. **Kellermann AL; Rivara FP**, *et al.* Validating survey responses to questions about gun ownership among owners of registered handguns. *Am J Epidemiol* 1990;131:1080–4.

16. **Australian Institute of Criminology**. *Australian Crime: Facts and Figures 2001.* Canberra: Australian Institute of

Criminology, 2002, 20. http://www.aic.gov.au/
publications/facts/2001/facts_and_figures_2001.pdf
(accessed 13 Nov 2006).

17. **Reuter P**, Mouzos J. Australia: a massive buyback of low-risk guns. In: Ludwig J, Cook P, eds. *Evaluating gun policy: effects on crime and violence.* Washington, DC: Brookings Institute, 2003:130.

18. **Mouzos J.** *Homicide in Australia. 2003–2004 National Homicide Monitoring Program (NHMP) Annual Report,* Research and Public Policy Series. Canberra: Australian Institute of Criminology, 2005:13.

19. **Minino AM**, Anderson RN, Fingerhut LA, *et al. Deaths: injuries, 2002, National Vital Statistics Reports.* Vol 54. Atlanta: National Center for Health Statistics, Centers for Disease Control and Prevention, 2006:32.

20. **Cockburn M**. Poll shows enormous support for total ban: AGB McNair. *Sydney Morning Herald.* Sydney, 6 May, 1996.

21. **Steketee M**. *Huge majority of voters supports bans: newspoll, The Australian.* Sydney, 7 May, 1996.

22. **Chapman S**. *Over our dead bodies. Port Arthur and Australia's fight for gun control.* Annandale: Pluto Press, 1998:61.

23. **Chan C**, Gordon M. Howard victory on gun bans. *Weekend Australian.* Sydney, 11 May, 1996.

24. **Chan G**, Shanahan D. Howard praises Ministers' decision. *Weekend Australian.* Sydney, 11 May, 1996.

25. **Millet M**. It's thumbs up. *Sydney Morning Herald.* Sydney, 1 Mar, 1997.

26. **Kreisfeld R**. *Indications of misclassification of causes of death,* Personal communication (e-mail to Chapman S). Adelaide: National Injury Surveillance Unit (NISU), 2006.

27. **Faltas S**, McDonald G, Waszink C. *Removing small arms from society: a review of weapons collection and destruction programmes.* Occasional paper no. 2. Geneva: Small Arms Survey, 2001, 4. http://www.smallarmssurvey.org/files/sas/publications/o_papers.html (Accessed 21 November 2006).

28. **Cantor C**, Mullen P, Alpers P. Mass homicide: the civil massacre. *J Am Acad Psychiatry Law* 2000;28:55–63.

29. **Fox J**, Levin J. Multiple homicide: patterns of serial and mass murder. *Crime Justice Abstr* 1998;23.

Sudan's Gun Buyback Programs Will Reduce Crime

Adiok Mayik

Adiok Mayik is a writer and Sudanese national who lives in the United States. In the following viewpoint, he argues in favor of a gun buyback program funded by the Sudanese government. He asserts that illicit small arms entered Sudan through the arming of national militias formed to combat rebellion during the Second Sudanese Civil War. Unfortunately, Mayik says, the guns remain and are being used to commit crimes. Mayik discourages Sudanese leaders from forcibly reclaiming the firearms and recommends a more civil exchange program.

As you read, consider the following questions:

1. From where did the tribal youths who composed the Sudanese national armies come?
2. What other African countries have faced disarmament problems like those of Sudan?
3. What three main challenges are ex-combatants facing now that the war is over, as stated by the author?

Sudan as a whole is and will continue to be in oddities from the post-conflict spilt over small arms and their misuse for quite some time. If we, however, inject some science in this scenario in order to define and justify this eccentricity, it

Adiok Mayik, "Buy Guns Back from Ex-Combatants and Civilians," *The New Sudan Vision*, May 24, 2009, pp. 1–5. Reproduced by permission of the publisher and author.

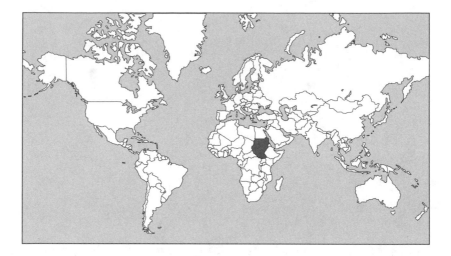

would be logical to see the inter-tribal small arms conflict as aftershock from the aftermath of the twenty-one years of a brutal war with each other. These definitions and many others will help us find the solutions to effectively disarm civilians and ex-combatants. Many people are troubled with many questions that produce fewer answers, when and how can we end this eccentricity in order to embark on reintegration and peaceful resettlement?

This is the question every Sudanese inside and outside Sudan is grappling with. This [viewpoint], therefore, looks at the dimensions and the extents of civilian armament in all corners of the Sudan. The [viewpoint] also evaluates exhausted methods of disarmament currently employed and will further explore opinions/suggestions of alternative means to obtain these guns without bloodshed from civilians who don't need them during the time we need peace.

The Spread of Small Arms

First, let me try to expose a few ways I know small arms got into many wrong hands all over the Sudan. The Government of Sudan used poor youth who flocked to northern towns as national armies to suppress the rebellion in the south as the war raged on since 1983.[1] The armament of these tribal youths as a powerful force was of paramount advantage to the government side. Their force helped balance out a war, which dragged on for twenty years with an eye for an eye, revenge for revenge, and retribution for the same in return. These tribal youths hailed from the impoverished villages of the Nuba Mountains, Darfur regions, northern and southern Kordofan regions, southern Blue Nile regions, some parts of southern Sudan, and eastern Sudan regions. Most of these youths must have been attracted to join several militias in the name of earning petty salaries in return. Others were coerced to join the military through conscriptions. Still others were promised free college education upon enlistment and after military services.

Although the SPLA/M [Sudan People's Liberation Army/Movement] in the south, on the other hand, used almost the same strategies to attract young and able-bodied men to pick up arms, none of its military personnel were paid any salary. This raised another question as to whether the arms race in south Sudan was purely out of patriotism. Of course, an equal force was applied from the southern side to balance the force from the northern government. Because the SPLA's military personnel were purely volunteers, the challenges to contain the extent of arms bearing were and are still huge even after the war. One of these challenges is how these guns were and are still being used these days. Another challenge is the record-keeping of the gun bearers. Then there is the problem of the deceased guerrilla fighters who inherited their guns. This later challenge haunts both parties of the war. Most of the atrocities and mistakes committed during the war were due to the fact that the SPLA soldiers used these guns to fight the war and to make a living like any other guerrilla movement. Lack

1. The Second Sudanese Civil War began in 1983 after President Gaafar Nimeiry attempted to create a federated Sudan by uniting the north and the south. The war ended in a cease-fire in 2005.

of compensation on the side of the SPLA rebellion at the time made it easy for young men in southern Sudan to go to war on their side to obtain guns.

Now the war has ended and with it comes the force of inertia. An unintended war is dragging on between the people themselves. How do both post-conflict governments get these guns back? It is the biggest challenge facing the north and south at the moment as these guns are now being used for something they were not intended for.

"Lack of compensation ... made it easy for young men in southern Sudan to go to war on their side to obtain guns."

Problems in North Sudan

Let me begin with challenges facing the north. The foundation of the Darfur rebellion used the government weapons obtained by youths who were ready to fight alongside them during the twenty-year-old war between north and south. These weapons, apart from their external supplements, were and still are being turned against the masters who provided them. The same occurred in eastern Sudan where the same guns were turned against the bosses. The same challenge, on the other hand, faces the south's semiautonomous authority.

Sudan is not the first country to face challenges like these, however. Post-conflict disarmament, demobilization, and reintegration of former combatants in Angola, Mozambique, Namibia, South Africa, and Zimbabwe had once been a bloody ordeal. However, these African countries are now peacefully enjoying the results of what they achieved in their conflicts: multiculturalism and economic equity. It is my opinion that the fruits of our civil wars will not be enjoyed for another century unless alternative and peaceful disarmament methods are designed to help address the problems of the post-conflict peace-building process.

The spillover of small arms in the hands of untrained civilians in Sudan must be seen as a vast regional problem that may subsequently affect lives in the neighboring countries. According to a report presented by the Human Rights Watch, in May 2002, hundreds of Sierra Leonean ex-combatants still cross into Liberia to fight as mercenaries, loot businesses, and attack as highway bandits. Sudan can easily fall prey into the same situation as it seeks to recover from a deeply rooted destruction of economy, social system, and human capitals.

> "The fruits of our civil wars will not be enjoyed for another century unless alternative and peaceful disarmament methods are designed."

The Government of Sudan is currently under the international pinch to disarm the Arab militias causing chaos in Darfur. Although the Arab tribes in Kordofan have done the Sudan government a great favor to help suppress the rebellion in Darfur, it is worth noting by token of plain truth that most leaders in Khartoum do not admire the proportion these weapons were used. The solution is simply to hide the embarrassment because how do you disarm someone on the loose; I mean someone who is not on your payroll? I am not saying the government did not arm these Arab militias in Kordofan who are causing terror in Darfur, don't quote me wrong here. I am simply saying here that most of the small arms Sudanese civilians bear were dispensed with great intentions by the authorities concerned, but the implications are now turning out to be too complicated for them to disentangle. The unintended consequences are huge.

Problems in South Sudan

The Government of Southern Sudan (GOSS) is entangled in its own, same maze. Most of the youths who were armed to fight the war did exactly what they were told to do by the

Map of Sudan

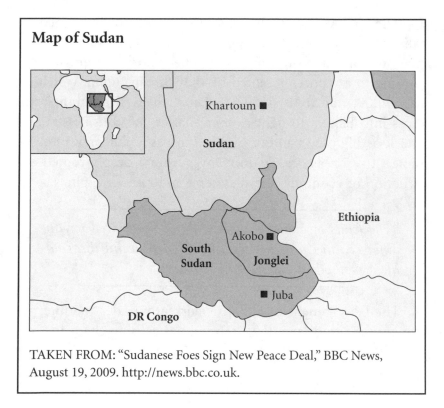

TAKEN FROM: "Sudanese Foes Sign New Peace Deal," BBC News, August 19, 2009. http://news.bbc.co.uk.

movement. However, they also did most of the things they were not told to do. For example, they were trained to stay in designated barracks with these weapons. Some of them stayed in barracks as told, but some did not. As a result, most guns ended up in the cattle camps where they were and still are used for cattle defense and hunting. The dangers are that the uses of these weapons turned bloody as cattle defense was extended into cattle rustling and hunting animals was extended into hunting members of other ethnic groups.

The episodes in the Jonglei state between the Lou Nuer and Dinka Duk, Lou Nuer and Murle, Dinka Bor and Murle, is a practical evidence of small arms proliferation allusion. The same loathes are observed between the Bull Nuer and Abiemnom Dinka of Unity state. Dinka Agar and neighboring ethnic groups of Lake state are in similar maze. The same situation applies in Warrap state between different sections of the Dinka, and the most recent observation between the Mundari and Bari in Central Equatoria is no exception. And finally but not the least, the frequent human hunt in Eastern Equatoria is the oldest of all of them.

All these aforementioned tribal conflicts are what I termed the unintended use of the small arms, which got into the hands of unemployed civilians. Now, how both the GOSS and the GNU [Government of National Unity] can get these guns back is the biggest subject of this [viewpoint]. There is no doubt that the Government of Southern Sudan has tried coercive disarmament without success. Instead, this coercive disarmament turns ugly and brutal as the former and self-disbanded ex-combatants who are mostly the bearers of illegal guns respond with similar force. This is practically evidenced in Lake state and Jonglei state where SPLA disarmament units clashed with armed civilians who were supposed to be disarmed.

"Using force to disarm civilians should be completely reserved as plan F."

Launching a Disarmament Program

Why not try an alternative method of disarmament? As most communities and civilians are settling back in peaceful post-conflict environment, the unemployed ex-combatants are definitely facing uncountable struggles to feed their families, obtain clothing, and send their children back to schools. Can the Government of Southern Sudan, Government of National Unity, and the NGOs [nongovernmental organizations] working alongside them launch a *gun buyback program?* It is my conviction and opinion that if programs like these are launched with legitimate transparency, honesty, and consistency, it is likely that most ex-combatants who are unemployed and armed can come forward to sell their guns in exchange for money. The lump sums they could earn out of these sales can be used on their own discretions. They may be informed to use the proceeds to start small retail businesses, send their children to college, buy cows, buy lands, etc.

As I mentioned earlier, small arms proliferation in Sudan is indeed our own problem, but a problem we share with the neighboring countries. Sudan can ask for hands from the neighboring countries. Say for example, Kenya, Uganda, Congo, Chad, and Egypt can set their own gun buyback programs and stations where armed civilians can opt to drop their guns off for cash. This, I presume, cannot bear fruits in one [day], one week, a month, a year, two years, or even a few several years. It could be a gradual process, which may turn out lucrative on all ends.

The cost of having a well-armed civilian population such as this of Sudan is way more than the cost of buying these guns back honestly from them. Using force to disarm civilians should be completely reserved as plan F. It is easy for these armed civilians to turn into very strong commercial highway bandits and town robbers like what happened in Liberia and many countries of Southern Africa block, which have been out of war before us. It is also easy for these armed and unemployed youths to be used by discontented politicians to wage other unnecessary rebellions, which we have already seen happen in Darfur and in eastern Sudan. Coercive disarmament is not going to work and it will continue to cause a lot of deaths.

Periodical Bibliography

The following articles have been selected to supplement the diverse views presented in this chapter.

Chitra Ahanthem   "Time to Stop the Bullets, Kill the Gun?" *Kangla Online*, June 7, 2008. www.kanglaonline.com.

Pauline Dempers   "Global Week of Action Against Gun Violence to Disarm Domestic Violence," *Namibian*, June 19, 2009. www.namibian.com.na.

William Daniel Garst   "China's Strict Gun Laws Make Me Feel Safe," *Global Times*, August 12, 2009.

Gazette (Montreal)   "Letter: Guns Curtail Police Abuse," December 9, 2007.

Luke Harding   "Strict German Gun Laws Fail to Prevent School Shooting," *Guardian* (UK), March 11, 2009. www.guardian.co.uk.

William P. Hoar   "Mexican Violence, Gun Controls," *New American*, May 25, 2009.

National Post (Canada)   "Give Us Crime Prevention, Not Gun Control," November 12, 2009.

Tom Peterkin   "Finland School Shooting: Gun Laws Not Tightened Since Jokela Massacre," *Daily Telegraph* (UK), September 23, 2008. www.telegraph.co.uk.

Scotsman (Edinburgh)   "Tight Gun Control, but Still Germany Is Not Immune," March 12, 2009.

Jacob Sullum   "Drug Control Begets Gun Control," *Reason*, July 2009.

Jane Francis Lepawah Tansinda   "Cameroon: Combating Gun Related Violence," *Cameroon Tribune* (Yaoundé), June 29, 2009.

The Effects of Gun Ownership and Gun Control on Society

The Proliferation of Small Arms Is a Global Challenge

Thomas Jackson, Nicholas Marsh, Taylor Owen, and Anne Thurin

Thomas Jackson, Nicholas Marsh, and Anne Thurin work for the International Peace Research Institute in Oslo, Norway (PRIO). Taylor Owen is a doctoral scholar for the Canadian Social Sciences and Humanities Research Council with prior affiliations with PRIO. In the following viewpoint, the authors argue that the spread of small arms continues to be a worldwide problem. Firearms are used in countless homicides and suicides annually, and their presence continues to result in a number of human rights abuses, including threats to human dignity, human security, and human development. On both large and small scales, the authors assert, small arms are a significant cause of human suffering around the globe.

As you read, consider the following questions:

1. What was the number of homicides and suicides in Norway in 2003?

2. According to a 2001 report by Amnesty International, how many governments and non-state armed forces were using small arms to abuse human rights?

Thomas Jackson, Nicholas Marsh, Taylor Owen, and Anne Thurin, *Who Takes the Bullet? The Impact of Small Arms Violence*, Oslo, Norway: Norwegian Church Aid and International Peace Research Institute, 2005. Reproduced by permission.

3. As stated by the authors, what is the leading cause of death worldwide for people fifteen to forty-four years old?

Violence arising from the global proliferation and diffusion of small arms has been identified by many development agencies as a severe challenge to their humanitarian objectives. For example, in August 2004, the Norwegian Ministry of Foreign Affairs published a strategy document on development and peace-building. In a section entitled "Control of Small Arms and Light Weapons," the document states that:

> "Internal and smaller regional conflicts are often triggered and prolonged by ready access to small arms and light weapons. These weapons also fuel crime and violence, displace civilians and undermine humanitarian assistance. . . . In many regions of the world small arms and light weapons [SALW] constitute a serious threat to peace, reconciliation, safety, security and sustainable development."

The position held by Norway is mirrored by a wide variety of governments, international organisations and NGOs [non-governmental organisations].

The proliferation of small arms can be aptly described as a crisis because in many areas across the world high-powered weaponry is increasingly being diffused into communities. This flow of weapons has shown no sign of slowing down—every year millions of new weapons are produced and sold on world markets. Small arms violence will not be controlled easily—indeed after a decade of international attention it shows little sign of abating.

Human Dignity

Norwegian Church Aid's [NCA's] central task is to uphold human dignity. In real terms, this means that NCA will "uphold and protect human dignity by working on an agenda of human development, human rights and human security," motivated by a concern for human rights, human development, and human security. In particular, Norwegian Church Aid seeks to integrate these three pillars into all of its development work. The small arms crisis affects all three components of human dignity. The consequences of armed violence on human security, human rights, and human development are shown below.

"The proliferation of small arms can be aptly described as a crisis because in many areas across the world high-powered weaponry is increasingly being diffused into communities."

A human security perspective means a shift in focus from threats to the state, such as interstate war to threats to the individual. Small arms violence immediately becomes a key concern both as a primary human security threat and as a threat multiplier.

Today's reality is that most preventable premature mortality is not a result of interstate wars. In fact, disease, violence, natural disasters and civil conflict are the leading threats to human security as we enter the 21st century.

These figures [shown in the sidebar of this viewpoint] are taken from several different sources, and may well underestimate the extent of casualties. The 'disasters' figure is based upon information downloaded from the ... Office of [U.S.] Foreign Disaster Assistance (OFDA)/Center for Research on the Epidemiology of Disasters (CRED) International Disaster Database. War, homicide and suicide figures are taken from the WHO [World Health Organization] *World Report on Violence and Health*. The figure for war includes indirect casualties as well as battle deaths. In many countries, especially in the developed world, suicides far outnumber homicides. For example, in Norway during 2003, there were 502 suicides and 44 homicides. The figure for communicable disease is taken from the WHO's *World Health Report 2001*.

The human security approach recommends the protection of the individual as well as the state, and in so doing encompasses a wide range of internal nonmilitary threats.

Concerning small arms, as Don Hubert of the Canadian Ministry of Foreign Affairs [Foreign Affairs and International Trade Canada] argues, using a human security approach does more than simply bring more issues to the security rubric. More fundamentally, it shifts the focus from the weapons to the safety and welfare of the individual:

> "Reducing the number of arms is a means to an end rather than an end in itself—the real objective is not just fewer guns but safer people."

Awareness of the numerous threats to the individual has prompted a substantial shift in relevant security issues and thinking. For development and humanitarian aid organisations, adopting a human security approach is critical, for it is at the local, human level that they can work to mitigate the effects of small arms violence.

For many years, human rights organisations have reported on the relationships between small arms misuse and serious violations of human rights. While governments and international organisations have repeatedly spelled out their concerns, Amnesty International in particular has continued to highlight transfers of arms to parties that use them to commit serious human rights violations.

For example, a 2001 report by Amnesty International calculated that in at least 100 states, governments and non-state armed forces were using small arms and light weapons to abuse human rights and break international humanitarian law. As a report by Oxfam [International] and Amnesty International for the Control Arms Campaign points out, small arms:

> "play a key role in perpetrating abuses of international human rights and humanitarian law—through their direct use

or through the threat of use. More injuries, deaths, displacements, rapes, kidnappings and acts of torture are inflicted or perpetrated with small arms than with any other type of weapon."

The importance of highlighting the links between small arms violence and human rights violations was confirmed with the appointment of Barbara Frey as the UN Special Rapporteur on the prevention of human rights violations committed with small arms and light weapons.

This report highlights the ways that small arms violence often prevents humanitarian and development organisations from achieving their objectives. The most direct impact of small arms violence on development is the death and injury of hundreds of thousands of people. In addition, there are indirect effects that have a much wider range. These include:

- Violent crime

- Collapse of health and education services

- Damage to infrastructure

- Displacement of people fleeing violence

- Declining economic activity

- Preventing development assistance . . .

Small Arms as a Violence Multiplier

Armed violence is not the same as violence. The addition of weapons to a violent situation can dramatically increase its lethality. Knives are much more deadly than fists, and guns are much more fatal than knives. As an example, one study of hospital admissions in Australia found that the mortality rate of gunshot wounds was some 100 percent higher than stabbings.

Violence is, and has always been, a part of societies across the world. The role of guns is to dramatically intensify this violence. With a firearm, such as a pistol, a single gunshot wound can prove fatal, and a person can kill many people around him. It is very hard to run away from a gun, and almost impossible for an unarmed person to defend himself. Often, the response to a threat by others using guns is for the threatened to acquire small arms of their own.

The threat of their use can be enough to instil fear. This fear can be used to intimidate political opponents, to commit crimes with impunity, to silence the victims of sexual abuses or domestic violence.

"The addition of weapons to a violent situation can dramatically increase its lethality."

This role of small arms as a multiplier was pointed out in a document entitled *Tackling Poverty by Reducing Armed Violence* produced by the UK's [United Kingdom's] Department for International Development (DFID):

> "Although SALW are rarely the root cause of conflict, crime or insecurity, their wide availability acts as a 'multiplier of violence', making conflict more lethal, crime more violent and people's lives, assets and livelihoods more insecure. . . . By increasing the risk of armed violence, SALW availability can obstruct and raise the costs of development and humanitarian aid in areas where these are desperately needed. Virtually all sectors of society can be badly affected, but the impact on the poor and the marginalised tends to be most traumatic."

The role of small arms as a multiplier means that there is not a direct relationship between the number of guns in a society and its propensity to violence. However, when mixed with other factors, the addition of small arms can, quite literally, be explosive. Such risk factors include communities that also suffer from:

- Little or no effective law enforcement

- Cultures in which disputes are settled through violence

- An association between masculinity and violence

- Powerful criminal gangs

- High levels of poverty and social inequality

As a multiplier of violence, small arms can also contribute to social deterioration. Small arms are instruments that provide their possessor with power—literally the power of life and death. They can then be used to erode (or destroy) traditional social norms, values and relationships.

For example, in Uganda Oxfam has noted, "the possession of small arms has greatly affected the power relationships within families. Sons with guns rarely obey parents and elders. The gun—especially in rural pastoral Kotido—settles feuds and personal vendettas." Once the possessor of a gun realises its power, he can become aware that laws and customs prohibiting murder, robbery, trafficking, assault, or rape can be ignored.

While effective police and law enforcement can attempt to slow down the influx and impact of weapons, in many developing regions of the world, mitigating mechanisms and institutions are overwhelmed by the rising tide of violence. . . .

"Small arms are instruments that provide their possessor with power—literally the power of life and death."

Armed Violence Disproportionately Affects the Developing World

The 2003 World Bank publication *Breaking the Conflict Trap* notes that countries with economically marginalised economies (with low incomes, economic decline and reliance upon commodity exports) have a tenfold higher risk of being in-

Leading Threats to Human Security

Global Death Registry, 2000

Cause of Death	Global Estimate
Disasters	55,000
War	310,000
Homicide	520,000
Suicide	850,000
Communicable Disease	17,777,000

Thomas Jackson,
Who Takes the Bullet?
The Impact of Small Arms Violence, *2005.*

volved in civil conflict than their more successful neighbours. . . . This risk of war is mirrored by the concentration of firearm violence in developing countries.

Not only are there vastly more small arms deaths in the developing world than in the developed world, the impact of these casualties, as well as the *de facto* effects of the presence of these guns, are both far greater in poorer nations.

Put another way, a gun in Rio de Janeiro is likely to have a greater societal impact than one in Oslo. This discrepancy is due to the lack of policing, health care and social limits on violence in Rio that are found in Oslo.

Development policy makers and workers are uniquely placed to tackle many aspects of the small arms crisis. Armed violence, whose effects are felt widely and indiscriminately around the world, should no longer be regarded as a simple security issue, but more importantly as a threat to human dignity, human security, human rights and development. . . .

The Global Epidemic of Small Arms Violence

The 2002 *World Report on Violence and Health* published by the World Health Organization (WHO) states that the impacts of violence:

> ". . . can be seen, in various forms, in all parts of the world. Each year, more than a million people lose their lives, and many more suffer nonfatal injuries, as a result of self-inflicted, interpersonal or collective violence. Overall, violence is among the leading causes of death worldwide for people aged 15–44 years.

> Although precise estimates are difficult to obtain, the cost of violence translates into billions of US dollars in annual health care expenditures worldwide, and billions more for national economies in terms of days lost from work, law enforcement and lost investment."

There are, of course, many causes of violence. In its 2002 report, the WHO listed the risk factors as being "prevailing cultural norms, poverty, social isolation and such factors as alcohol abuse, substance abuse *and access to firearms.*"

In 2003, the WHO noted that the "availability of small arms and light weapons is an important factor in increasing the lethality of violent situations." In particular, if large numbers of guns are added to preexisting cultures of violence, poverty, exclusion, or alcohol and narcotic abuse, the consequences can be lethal. . . .

Whether one is concerned with domestic homicide in the USA, urban violence in Guatemala, pastoral conflict in Uganda, or civil war in Nepal, one factor remains salient: The role of small arms and light weapons is a common tool of violence.

Gun-Related Crimes Are Costly for the People of New Zealand

Amanda Ruler

In the following viewpoint, Amanda Ruler, the South Australian branch coordinator for the Medical Association for Prevention of War, argues that gun law reform is necessary in New Zealand because of the enormous toll firearm crimes are taking on the economy and the well-being of the people. She notes that the rates of homicides and suicides declined after Australia passed tougher firearms legislation and uses this data to urge that New Zealand do the same. Ultimately, she advocates for stricter gun control policies worldwide.

As you read, consider the following questions:

1. According to Ruler, on average how much did a single homicide cost the people of New Zealand in 2004?
2. About how many guns are in New Zealand?
3. About how many small arms and light weapons are there worldwide?

The gun death rates in New Zealand from suicide and homicide are considerably higher than in Australia. In 2005, these gun death rates per 100,000 people were .91 in Australia

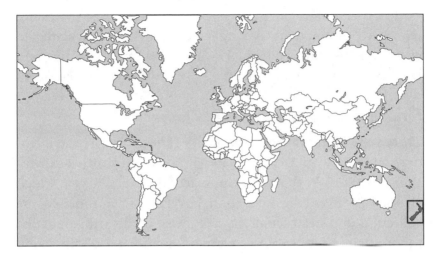

and 1.3 in New Zealand. Are the higher death rates in New Zealand a result of your country's relatively relaxed laws in relation to gun ownership? Apart from exceptions such as pistols, military-style semiautomatic firearms and restricted weapons, New Zealand legislation does not require firearms to be registered.

"Interpersonal violence is expensive."

In Australia in 2005, 15 percent of homicide victims were killed with firearms. Of firearms that were used, 90 percent were unregistered, and only 13 percent of offenders were licensed to use the firearm. Over one-third of the solved firearm homicides occurred between friends and acquaintances (35 percent) and a further 26 percent between intimate partners. Family members were responsible for 15 percent of firearm homicides, while fewer than 7 percent involved strangers. Overall, women are more likely to be killed by an intimate partner (48 percent) or a family member (23 percent). Of these, 19 percent of female victims were more likely to be killed with a firearm by a male partner. Similar findings have been described in New Zealand.

Interpersonal violence is expensive. Economic losses are related to productivity. A single homicide was calculated to cost in 2004, on average, US$602,000 in Australia, and US$829,000 in New Zealand.

Stricter Gun Laws

There were 13 mass shootings in the 18 years before the introduction of new gun control laws in 1996 in Australia. In response to the Port Arthur massacre in April 1996, which claimed 35 lives, the Australian government authorised the collection and destruction of categories of firearms designed to kill many times over, i.e., semiautomatic and pump-action rifles and shotguns. In total, more than 700,000 guns were removed and destroyed from an adult population of about 12.3 million. Newly prohibited were semiautomatic and pump-action rifles and shotguns. Australia's revised gun laws also required all firearms to be individually registered to their licensed owners, prohibited private firearm sales, and required that each gun transfer through a licensed arms dealer be approved only after the police were satisfied of a genuine reason for ownership. Possession of firearms for self-defence in Australia is specifically prohibited and few civilians are licensed to possess handguns. All Australian governments have agreed that firearm possession is not a right but a conditional privilege. Genuine reason must be shown for owning a firearm and self-defence is not a recognised reason.

New Zealand has about one million guns among its population of four million people and the majority of these arms are claimed to be used for hunting and sporting purposes. While the category of firearms which must be registered in New Zealand does not extend to sporting rifles or shotguns, civilians wanting to possess these firearms must be 16 years of age and are subject to a vetting and licensing regime. Like the Australian government, the New Zealand High Court has declared that there is no general right to bear arms.

After the Aramoana massacre in New Zealand [during which a thirty-three-year-old man killed thirteen people with a semiautomatic rifle], in November 1990, the government substantially tightened gun laws generally. The laws were passed in 1992 and stipulated that: written permits were required to order guns or ammunition by mail-order; ammunition sales were restricted to firearms license holders; photographs were added to firearms licenses; license holders were required to have secure storage for firearms at their homes; and all license holders had to be re-vetted for new licenses, valid for only 10 years. The law also created the new category of "military-style semiautomatic", which mainly covered the appearance rather than the functionality of the guns. These required a special endorsement, security and registration in the same manner as pistols.

A study, which examined firearms legislation and reductions in firearm-related suicide deaths in New Zealand, looked at the impact of introducing more restrictive firearms legislation through the Arms Amendment Act 1992. National suicide data was examined for eight years before and ten years after the introduction of the legislation. Results found that after legislation, the mean annual rate of firearm-related suicides decreased by 46 percent for the total population. Following the introduction of legislation restricting ownership and access to firearms, firearm-related suicides significantly decreased, particularly among youth.

These findings are supported by another study which found that the proportion of firearm suicides decreased simultaneously with the proportion of households owning firearms. These results are in line with the well-established association between availability of firearms at home and risk of firearm suicide, and tend to confirm the argument that removal of rapid-firing firearms may more substantially reduce the risk of suicide.

Gun Control Reforms Fall Short

Despite these reforms, New Zealand's gun-related death rate remains much higher than Australia's, so the question must be asked whether the reforms go far enough. Using an observational study of official statistics, researchers carried out a study of changes in firearm death rates and compared trends in pre– and post–gun law reform firearm-related mass killings in Australia between 1979 and 2003. The main outcome measures were changes in trends of total firearm death rates, mass fatal shooting incidents, rates of firearm homicide, suicide and unintentional firearm deaths, and of total homicides and suicides per 100,000 of the population. The rates per 100,000 of the population's total firearm deaths, firearm homicides and firearm suicides all at least doubled their existing rates of decline, after the revised gun laws. In conclusion, Australia's 1996 gun law reforms were followed by more than a decade free of fatal mass shootings, and accelerated declines in firearm deaths, particularly suicides. Total homicide rates followed the same pattern. Removing large numbers of rapid-firing firearms from civilians may be an effective way of reducing mass shootings, and firearm homicides and suicides.

Should New Zealand follow Australia's lead and ban semi-automatic and pump-action rifles and shotguns in order to further reduce the impact of gun-related deaths?

"Removing large numbers of rapid-firing firearms from civilians may be an effective way of reducing mass shootings, and firearm homicides and suicides."

A study into the criminal use of firearms in New Zealand was based on a survey of 51 New Zealand prison inmates and focused on the acquisition and use of illegal firearms, in order to obtain information about patterns of firearms ownership within the criminal community. Findings confirmed the existence of a large pool of illegally held firearms in New Zealand

and that people could relatively easily obtain firearms of almost any type from within the criminal community.

A New Zealand report by former judge Thomas Thorp called for many new restrictions on legal gun ownership, including banning various features, and, particularly unpopular among firearm owners, that all guns be registered. The National Government in 1999, its last year in office, introduced an Arms Amendment Bill (No 2) to implement the recommendations but the bill was withdrawn due to the opposition. The government then introduced a much-reduced Arms Amendment Bill (No 3), which increased penalties for distribution, manufacture and use of illegal weapons. It has been in the Select Committee since 2005, and while there has been much debate about proceeding with it, the government has not initiated any firm steps.

International Firearm Legislation

Internationally, the situation regarding gun-related deaths is grim. Former United Nations Secretary-General Kofi Annan, has stated: "Small arms have damaged development prospects and imperilled human security in every way. Indeed, there is probably no single tool of conflict so widespread, so easily available and so difficult to restrict as small arms."

"Gun control is an issue of national and international importance as it profoundly affects the security and health and well-being of all people."

There are about 600 million small arms and light weapons (SALW) worldwide. These weapons kill an estimated 1,000 people per day, the majority of whom are civilians. The global trade in small arms is estimated to be worth about US$4 billion, of which a quarter is considered illicit or is not recorded, as required by law.

The Port Arthur Massacre

Australians reacted with horror and outrage when, on a Sunday evening in [April] 1996, they learned from their televisions that over 30 people had been murdered and many others injured in an orgy of violence in the Port Arthur Historic Site (PAHS), Tasmania, one [of] the nation's most venerable historical sites, and adjacent locations. They were told that the atrocities had been perpetrated by a young Caucasian man with pale skin and long white hair brandishing a military rifle—a kind of quasi-albino Rambo—who apparently had a dislike of Japanese tourists.

In summary, the story delivered to the breathless world was that shortly before 1:30 P.M. that cloudless Sunday afternoon, the gunman had entered the Broad Arrow Café at the PAHS and picked off, with unfathomable callousness, one tourist after another. He killed a number of other individuals as he exited the PAHS and holed himself up in a nearby tourist guest house, the Seascape, in a siege that only ended when he burned the building down the following morning (an event that was seen shortly afterwards on television).

Carl Wernerhoff,
"A Critical Study of the Port Arthur Massacre," 2006.
www.loveforlife.com.au.

The Programme of Action [to Prevent, Combat and Eradicate the Illicit Trade in Small Arms and Light Weapons in All Its Aspects] devised by the United Nations, which was agreed in July 2001, provides a non-legally binding framework for members to adopt various measures to combat the illicit trade in small arms and light weapons nationally, regionally and internationally. The Firearms Protocol criminalises the illicit trafficking in and manufacture of firearms, and requires measures such as the marking and tracing of firearms to be put in place. A politically binding instrument to enable states to identify and trace illicit SALW was adopted by the United Nations in 2005.

An initiative that is currently being discussed internationally is a possible arms treaty. Such a treaty would cover the trade not only of small arms, but also of all conventional weapons, e.g., tanks and fighter aircraft. Its purpose would be to prevent weapons from being transferred to countries where they may be used to violate international law and human rights.

Gun control is an issue of national and international importance as it profoundly affects the security and health and well-being of all people, thus it is also an important issue for all health professionals. All weapons, whether they are small arms or more conventional tanks and missiles, are lethal, and alternatives to violent conflict must be sought and developed to ensure a more peaceful, safe and secure world.

Jamaican Gun Ownership Is a Threat to Children and Adolescents

Arthur Williams

Arthur Williams is the minister of state in Jamaica. In the following viewpoint, he argues that Jamaican children are not only being shot in gun-related crimes, but many of them have become gunmen in their own right. Unfortunately, the caretakers of scores of children have been gunned down as well, leaving the next generation uncared for. Williams asserts that Jamaica has made some advances in the fight against gun violence in the past several decades, but much more needs to be done.

As you read, consider the following questions:

1. How many children were murdered in Jamaica in 2007?
2. What is a "shotta"?
3. How many firearms were seized by the police in Jamaica in 2007?

Violence, especially by the illegal gun, has for some time now, been driving fear in the hearts of Jamaicans, tarnishing the nation's image and retarding its development. All this has had a devastating impact on our children and their communities.

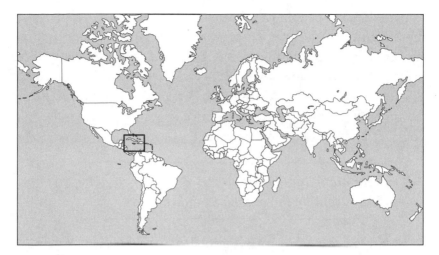

There are many horror stories of innocent young lives snuffed out by the gunman's bullet. This has become too frequent in some communities, if not pervasive, nationally. Painfully aware of this, and determined to continue to do something to change it, the Violence Prevention Alliance, the United Nations Development Programme, UNICEF (the United Nations Children's Fund) and the Ministry of National Security, are hosting this timely two-day consultation on "Reducing the Impact of Small Arms and Light Weapons on Children and Their Communities" [May 5, 2008].

The wanton use of illegal guns is a clear and present danger to the Jamaican society, because they terrorize and traumatize our children and the communities in which they live, go to school, or have to pass through in their routine daily activities.

Guns Affect Children Everywhere

Statistics from the Jamaica Constabulary [Force] show that in 2007, a total of 65 children were murdered. That is more than five per month, more than one per week. In 2006, it was the same number, 65; in 2005 it was even higher—89. This is unacceptable.

In all 1,574 people were murdered in 2007, a total of 1,241 by the gun. In 2006, a total of 1,008 people were murdered by the gun; in 2005, the figure was 1,277. In addition, the police were called on to investigate 1,441 cases of shooting in 2007; 1,341 in 2006 and 1,646 in 2005. For a country with a population as small as ours, the incidence of gun violence defies all logic. It just does not make sense.

"There are many horror stories of innocent young lives snuffed about by the gunman's bullet."

Many of the 3,326 people murdered by the gun in the last three years in Jamaica were fathers, mothers, grandparents and guardians, and more often than not, the sole breadwinners for their children and other members of their families. You can therefore understand the devastating effect their deaths have had on the children they left behind, un-provided for, without the comfort of loving arms, tolerant and attentive ears and wise counsel to steer them along the narrow paths of life.

And the impact of gun violence on children goes far beyond the human toll, as children don't have to be hurt themselves to suffer extensive negative effects which go far beyond their initial grief. The trauma is even more devastating when the gun violence occurs at or near schools or in communities, as in these cases, it affects a large number of children, thereby spreading the trauma.

We have even had the experience here in some inner cities where schools have had to be closed for weeks on end because of gun violence. And rarely is there ever any psychological counseling available to these children who sometimes have to dodge bullets instead of happily skipping on their way to school.

The result is that thousands of children have had their lives of hope and promise and accomplishment deflected, even terminated, by the gun. The emotional and psychological impact of the tragedies often leave many children fighting a losing battle in trying to erase the emotional scars from which they suffer. Many are thrown off their original career paths, with their once-promising future ending in disaster.

Gun violence contributes in another significant way to the destruction of the lives of children. Living what they learn, some of these children in gun-infested communities become inured to gun violence from an early age. The apprenticeship of some children as young gunmen or "shottas", begin early in certain inner-city communities, where they are recruited as gangsters at a tender age, by the lure of the power of the gun.

"Thousands of children have had their lives of hope and promise and accomplishment deflected, even terminated, by the gun."

Preventing Gun Smuggling

Of course, gun violence, particularly as it affects children, is of paramount concern to the government, to NGOs [nongovernmental organizations] and indeed to civil society as a whole. Successive administrations have tried to tackle it from several angles, but it is a very complex problem, which requires multiple approaches. To reduce the threat it poses, a major and continuing initiative has to focus on preventing illegal guns from coming into the island. But, that is no easy task. In 2007, the police seized 648 firearms—ranging from rifles and submachine guns to semiautomatic pistols and revolvers. The police have been even more aggressive in their seizure of illegal guns since the start of 2008, but still the guns continue to turn up on our streets. Illegal guns are far too prevalent and easily available in Jamaica, and herein lies our problem.

Successive Jamaican governments have done much to halt the smuggling of guns into Jamaica. They have signed the relevant treaties such as the Inter-American Convention Against

Illicit Manufacturing of and Trafficking in Firearms, Ammunition, Explosives, and Other Related Materials [CIFTA], as well as a gun and drug interdiction agreement with the United States.

But the security forces do not have enough boats and planes and manpower to police our coastline—which is all of 1,022 kilometers long. Neither do the security forces have the resources to constantly monitor the more than 100 clandestine airstrips that are used by planes bringing in guns when they come to take out shipments of ganja [marijuana].

The truth is that the Jamaican coastline, in the absence of the adequate coast guard vessels, is a drug smugglers' dream. Guns are smuggled in also on fishing boats from Central America and aboard go-fast boats from South America. Gun smuggling and drug trafficking go hand in hand. Guns are needed to guard large stashes of drugs and cash. Drug traffickers use guns to keep their rivals at bay or to intimidate or murder those people who they cannot corrupt. So what have we been doing in Jamaica about the impact that gun violence is having on our children?

Current Gun Control Measures

As far back as 1974 the government of the day enacted a drastic and Draconian law—the Gun Court Act—to dissuade the smuggling and use in Jamaica of illegal guns.

Today, the Jamaica Constabulary [Force] has a Caribbean Search Unit, which is specially equipped and particularly adept at searching for illegal guns. It reaps success from time to time, but still illegal guns appear too frequently and just about everywhere.

As recently as last November [2007], a National Train-the-Trainers Course on the Control of the Legal Trade and Prevention of Illicit Trafficking in Firearms, Their Parts, and Ammunition, was held here.

The Jamaican Gun Court

The Gun Court was established on April 2, 1974, as an extension of the Supreme Court; with a decentralized structure, it has four provincial courts, as well as being present in the capital, Kingston. The Gun Court was created with the objective of making dealing with arms-related cases more agile and effective, in order to combat the incidence of armed violence which was increasing at a galloping rate.

The Gun Court operates without a jury, thus making it much swifter than an ordinary court. The court has authority in cases of illegal possession of arms and munitions, as well as in cases of armed attacks and shoot-outs. The only exception to firearms-related acts are homicides since according to Jamaican law, these trials must be by jury.

Daniel Luz, "Gun Courts,"
Comunidade Segura, May 6, 2007.

And then there is the work of the Violence Prevention Alliance, which is indeed tangible evidence of the sense of responsibility it displays towards the society, by its efforts to redeem troubled, violent communities—get rid of the guns—and make them safe again for the peace and prosperity and peace of mind of all citizens. But the alliance does not stop there.

"There have been a range of other responses to the impact that gun violence has on children and their communities in Jamaica."

By its actions, it emphasizes that crime and violence must never be acceptable, and that everybody in this country must take a stand and exercise their concerted responsibility to stamp it out whenever and wherever it rears its head.

There have been a range of other responses to the impact that gun violence has on children and their communities in Jamaica. Some have been legislative, others have been undertaken by the private sector, sometimes in co-operation with the government.

The Jamaica Constabulary [Force] launched its "Operation KingFish" task force in 2004 to focus on the apprehension and prosecution of leaders and members of organized criminal gangs here in Jamaica.

Also playing a critical role in curbing the flow of illegal guns and drugs into the island, is the border control strategy, which involves collaboration among various arms of the security forces. Your two-day consultation, which begins now, highlights your recognition of the fact that the government alone cannot bring about the changes that are so desperately and urgently needed. I am sure that it will achieve its goal of identifying best practices in the Caribbean and Central America that could help Jamaica and other countries in the region develop policies and programmes for reducing the impact of guns on children and their communities.

The most sustainable programmes will be those which are based on international frameworks, and recommendations from studies such as . . . "The Impact of Small Arms on Children and Adolescents in Central America and the Caribbean: A Case Study of El Salvador, Guatemala, Jamaica and Trinidad and Tobago", and lessons learnt from country experiences. . . .

To achieve this, not only must the flow of illegal guns in Jamaica be choked off, but there must be focus on the need to tackle economic inequality and social decay, as violence often has it roots in economic deprivation and social desperation.

Gun Ownership Is Not a Threat to Children's Rights

Michael Farris

Michael Farris is the chancellor and constitutional law professor at Patrick Henry College in Purcellville, Virginia. In the following viewpoint, he argues that the United States must not ratify the United Nations Convention on the Rights of the Child (UNCRC). He asserts that doing so would strip American gun owners of their rights. He also insists that gun ownership is not a threat to children in the way that the UNCRC claims. Instead, he says, the UNCRC will only threaten the well-being of law-abiding Americans and their families.

As you read, consider the following questions:

1. According to the author, which three rights are threatened by the UNCRC?
2. According to the author, what two conclusions can be drawn from the main assertions of the UNCRC?
3. How does the World Congress on Disarmament Education define "disarmament", as stated by the author?

Parental rights, religious rights, educational rights and the right to discipline are all threatened by the UN [United Nations] Convention on the Rights of the Child. But a careful review of the United Nations' own documents reveals an additional threat to the rights of Americans—the right of private gun ownership.

At first glance, the UN's discussion of guns and children focuses on the subject of children being improperly used by third world nations as child soldiers. All that can be said on this subject is that the UN Convention on the Rights of the Child, or UNCRC [also CRC], has had precious little impact in stopping this barbaric practice.

Yet there is another theme to be found in the UN's attack on guns.

UN child's rights advocates believe, teach and promote the idea that all private gun ownership is dangerous for children, and children have the *right* to grow up in a community that is free from all guns.

UNICEF's Agenda

Limiting the rights of gun ownership is not some secret agenda of the UN but is open for all to see. UNICEF [the United Nations Children's Fund], the official UN agency charged with the worldwide advancement of children's rights, has published a four-color brochure entitled: *No Guns Please, We Are Children.*

Inside this brochure we find the following assertions about guns and children:

- Small arms and light weapons kill and disable more children and adults than any other instrument of violence in conflict and post-conflict situations and on the streets of cities worldwide. Every year, deaths linked to small arms and light weapons run into the hundreds of thousands, with those injured exceeding 1 million.

- Small arms and light weapons cause profound physical and emotional damage, particularly to children, and affect their welfare.

- In societies destabilized by the use of small arms and light weapons, children are denied many of their human rights, including their rights to freedom from violence and exploitation, survival and development, health care, education, and care within a family environment. As a result, hard-won developmental gains are often lost and may even be reversed.

- In communities enjoying relative peace, children witness and are traumatized by the use of small arms and light weapons in domestic violence and in disputes. Children also become accidental victims because adults fail to keep the weapons out of their reach.

Two crucial conclusions can be drawn from these assertions:

First, the UN intends to address far more than children in war; the object is to eliminate the "threat" posed by guns from the lives of all children whether their community is characterized as "in conflict," "post-conflict," "destabilized," or "enjoying relative peace." Guns are a threat "on the streets of cities worldwide."

Second, the UN contends that the threat posed by guns violates the "human rights" of children.

This official UN brochure has more to say about the public policy implications of the demand for restrictions on firearms in the name of the human rights of children:

- "Efforts must be ongoing to overcome the destructive messages that small arms and light weapons are essential instruments for survival and protection in daily life."

- "Governments must support communities in eliminating the insecurity, fear and instability that often lead people to acquire and keep guns."

- "Regulations are needed to ensure that small arms and light weapons are not easy to acquire and are never accessible to children."

The UN believes the idea that small arms are "essential instruments for survival and protection" is a destructive attitude that violates the "respect for human rights" required by the UNCRC.

"The UN agenda for children does not stop with the direct disarming of individuals."

Other UN Propositions

In another United Nations official publication (*Guide to the Implementation of the World Programme of Action for Youth*), the UN urges member nations to "explore enacting bans on all handguns to civilians or certain cheap models that are attractive to youth."

The UN agenda for children does not stop with the direct disarming of individuals. Article 29 of the UN Convention on the Rights of the Child imposes educational standards on nations that become parties to the treaty. This includes "peace education," which in other UN contexts means disarmament education. The UN World Congress on Disarmament Education adopted the following statements:

Definition of disarmament

For the purposes of disarmament education, disarmament may be understood as any form of action aimed at limiting, controlling or reducing arms, including unilateral disarmament initiatives and, ultimately, general and complete disarmament under effective international control. It may also be understood as a process aimed at transforming the current system of armed nation states into a new world order of planned unarmed peace, in which war is no longer an in-

Ten Things to Know About the UN Convention on the Rights of the Child [CRC]

1. It is a treaty which creates binding rules of law. . . .

2. Its effect would be binding on American families, courts . . .

3. Children of other nations would not be impacted or helped in any direct way by our ratification.

4. The CRC would . . . override almost all American laws on children and families because of the U.S. Constitution's Supremacy Clause in Article VI.

5. The CRC has some elements that are self-executing, while others would require implementing legislation. Federal courts would have the power to determine which provisions were self-executing.

6. The courts would have the power to directly enforce the provisions that are self-executing.

7. Congress would have the power to directly legislate on all subjects necessary to comply with the treaty. This would [be] the most massive shift of power from the states to the federal government in American history.

8. A committee of 18 experts from other nations . . . has the authority to issue official interpretations of the treaty which are entitled to binding weight in American courts. . . .

9. Under international law, the treaty overrides even our Constitution.

10. Reservations . . . intended to modify our duty to comply with this treaty will be void if [deemed] inconsistent with the . . . purpose of the treaty.

Michael Farris, "Nannies in Blue Berets:
Understanding the UN Convention on the Rights of the Child,"
Parentalrights.org, December 15, 2008.

strument of national policy and peoples determine their own future and live in security based on justice and solidarity.

While our Second Amendment should be interpreted broadly to protect gun ownership, there is significant reason to believe that pressure will be placed on legislative bodies to tell adults that, while they may still own guns, they must be kept in another location if children are present in the home.

"The UN Convention on the Rights of the Child must be defeated."

The UN is not content with regulating our families and children. They want us to march into a New World Order without weapons. Our families and our means of defending our families are in significant peril.

The UN Convention on the Rights of the Child must be defeated.

Gun Confiscation by Uganda's National Army Has Violated Human Rights in the Karamoja Region

Human Rights Watch

In the following viewpoint, Human Rights Watch (HRW), a nonprofit organization dedicated to defending and protecting human rights, argues that the Ugandan army has abused the people of the Karamoja region of the country in its efforts to seize firearms. These abuses include torture, killings, detention, theft, and destruction of property. Although the government of Uganda has taken steps to stop such abuses, HRW asserts that much more could be done. In addition to preventing future abuses, HRW recommends that the Ugandan government punish those persons who have committed such violations in past disarmament campaigns.

As you read, consider the following questions:

1. In what year did the Ugandan army renew its program of forced disarmament?
2. Since 2001, how many firearms have been collected by the Ugandan army in the Karamoja region?

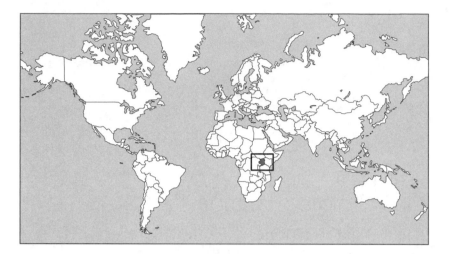

3. What steps has the Ugandan government taken to respond to human rights abuses during the forced disarmament campaigns?

In the remote Karamoja region of northeastern Uganda, pastoralist herding communities struggle for survival amidst frequent drought, intercommunal cattle raids, and banditry. Gun ownership is pervasive, and armed criminality and cattle raiding by civilians in Karamoja exposes the population there, as well as those in neighboring districts, to high levels of violence, and restricts even the movement of humanitarian workers. It poses significant challenges to the government's responsibility to provide for its citizens' security and human rights.

Uganda's Disarmament Campaigns

Since May 2006 the national army, tasked with law enforcement responsibilities in the region in the absence of an adequate police presence, renewed a program of forced disarmament to curb the proliferation of small arms. In so-called cordon and search disarmament operations, soldiers surround villages in the middle of the night and at daybreak force families outside while their houses are searched for weapons.

This report, based primarily on field research in Kampala and in the Kaabong and Moroto districts of the Karamoja region in January and February 2007 and additionally drawing on reporting by the United Nations (UN) and other sources, documents alleged human rights violations by soldiers of Uganda's army, the Uganda People's Defence Forces (UPDF), in cordon and search disarmament and other law enforcement operations in the region. These violations have included unlawful killings, torture and ill-treatment, arbitrary detention, and theft and destruction of property. While the Ugandan government has a legitimate interest in improving law and order in Karamoja, including stemming the proliferation of illegal weapons, it must do so in a manner consistent with human rights.

"The Ugandan government . . . has not adequately held to account those responsible for past abuses."

Human Rights Watch welcomes steps taken by the Ugandan government in the past year to curb such human rights violations during disarmament and other law enforcement operations, in response to international and domestic pressure. The Ugandan government, however, has not adequately held to account those responsible for past abuses, and allegations of human rights violations continue to surface periodically in connection with disarmament and other law enforcement operations in Karamoja.

The government has mounted several disarmament campaigns—some voluntary, some forced—in Karamoja since 2001 to collect what it now estimates to be as many as 30,000 unlawfully held weapons in the region. At the same time, however, government programs to improve security, including programs of disarmament, face a fundamental dilemma: Guns are used to defend from raiders as well as to rob and steal. The dynamics behind weapons possession in Karamoja include, for some, the desperate need to secure and defend their cattle and access to limited resources essential for their cattle, a matter of life and death. Removing weapons while not providing sufficient guarantees of safety and security renders, in their view, many communities vulnerable to attack.

Weak government institutions in the region exacerbate these vulnerabilities and leave law enforcement responsibilities in the hands of the UPDF. The present disarmament campaign is just one of these responsibilities, which also include recovering raided cattle, apprehending and prosecuting criminal suspects, and protecting livestock in UPDF-guarded enclosures.

"Soldiers routinely beat men, at times to uncover the location of weapons."

Cordon and Search Operations

In Kaabong district in December 2006 and January 2007, UPDF soldiers shot and killed 10 individuals, including three children, as they attempted to flee during cordon and search operations. Only one of the individuals killed was reported to have fired on the soldiers, while one other was running away with his gun. Four other individuals, including two children and one youth, were also shot and injured. In four armed confrontations with Karamojong communities between October 2006 and February 2007, at least two of which were preceded by cordon and search operations, dozens of civilians were killed, while the lives of an unknown number of UPDF soldiers were also claimed.

Soldiers routinely beat men, at times to uncover the location of weapons. In Moroto district victims of three cordon and search operations described an almost identical pattern of mass beatings by soldiers of the entire male population: Men were first rounded up outside of their homesteads, and then subjected to collective beatings with sticks, whips, guns, and tree branches accompanied by soldiers' demands that they "get the gun."

Following cordon and search operations, soldiers detained men in military facilities. Although one UPDF spokesperson described such detentions—purportedly for the purpose of inducing the surrender of weapons—as lasting no longer than 48 hours—Human Rights Watch interviewed some men who were detained without access to family members for at least two weeks. Former detainees reported to Human Rights Watch that military authorities subjected them to severe beatings and violent interrogations, along with deprivation of food, water, and adequate shelter.

Communities were also the victims of property destruction and theft. During one cordon and search operation, soldiers drove an armored personnel carrier through a homestead, crushing six homes, and narrowly missing a crowd of people.

"Allegations of human rights violations . . . have not ceased altogether."

By conducting cordon and search operations to seize weapons, rather than to prosecute firearms offenses, the government may be seeking to avoid legal requirements authorizing searches, arrests, and detentions in the context of law enforcement operations and that protect the rights of persons under national and international law. Consequently, post–cordon and search detentions lack judicial control, and, at times, are not specific to individuals suspected of criminal activity, thereby violating the rights to be free from arbitrary arrest and detention. Moreover, searches conducted during these operations are authorized by military order alone, and not court-issued warrants mandated under national law, violating individual privacy rights.

Responding to Human Rights Violations

In response to allegations of human rights violations during disarmament operations, the government of Uganda has taken several steps. These include launching four investigations; developing a set of internal UPDF guidelines governing the conduct of military personnel during cordon and search operations, the violation of which subjects a soldier to discipline under the UPDF Act; providing UPDF soldiers conducting cordon and search operations with human rights training; and engaging with community members and local leaders about the goals of disarmament.

These steps appear to have had an encouraging effect. The most recent information received by Human Rights Watch indicates that cordon and search operations, while still ongoing, have been markedly less violent than in earlier months of the disarmament campaign and accompanied by far fewer allegations of human rights violations. But allegations of human rights violations, most notably continued detention following cordon and search operations and isolated reports of beatings, have not ceased altogether. Moreover, none of the reports produced by government investigations has been made public. The Ugandan army wrote to Human Rights Watch in September 2007 that a number of soldiers have been brought to justice for human rights violations, but provided no details of the underlying offenses and punishments imposed. In the three explicitly disarmament-related cases of which Human Rights Watch is aware, soldiers were disciplined for petty theft.

Accordingly, although it has taken steps in the right direction, Human Rights Watch calls on the Ugandan government to make further progress in stopping human rights violations by its forces. It should end impunity for violations by its soldiers by investigating and prosecuting or disciplining abuses where appropriate, and safeguard against future violations by revising its disarmament policies to comply with its human rights obligations under national and international law.

Publicity garnered by the disarmament campaign has concentrated national and international attention on the challenges of survival and security in Karamoja; some of these challenges are imposed from within and some from without. The Ugandan government's efforts to respond to allegations of human rights violations in the past year have included increased engagement with the people of Karamoja, who have long been alienated from the rest of the country. To ensure the sustainability of efforts to bring security to the region, the Ugandan government, with the support of the international community and with the communities of Karamoja leading the way, should seize this opportunity to develop durable solutions that reduce conflict and reliance on guns for protection of lives and livelihoods in Karamoja.

The United Nations Gun Confiscation Program Violates Human Rights in East Africa

David B. Kopel, Paul Gallant, and Joanne D. Eisen

David B. Kopel is the research director, and Paul Gallant and Joanne D. Eisen are senior fellows at the Independence Institute, a nonprofit, nonpartisan Colorado organization that conducts public policy research. In the following viewpoint, the authors argue that the United Nations' attempts at forced disarmament in East Africa, specifically in Uganda and Kenya, have led to multiple human rights violations, including rape and murder. They recommend that future disarmament programs focus on the well-being of all citizens by offering education and some type of payback in exchange for small arms.

As you read, consider the following questions:

1. What is Operation NYUNDO?
2. By the end of the Ugandan genocide in 1979, how many people had been killed?
3. What other countries have faced human rights violations due to forced disarmament?

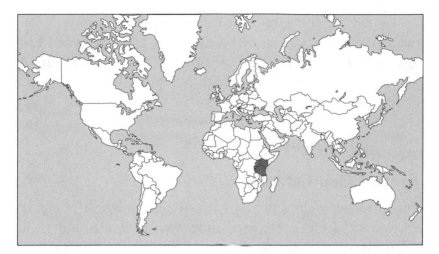

On June 26 [2006], the United Nations [UN] convened a major conference on gun control. Before demanding further control, the delegates ought to insist that the United Nations halt the use of torture, arson, and murder in the carrying out of existing UN gun control programs.

"The 'forcible disarmament' campaign has displaced tens and tens of thousands of people, turning them into starving refugees."

With United Nations support, the governments of Kenya and Uganda are attempting to confiscate all arms from the pastoral tribes of the Kenya-Uganda borderlands. The "forcible disarmament" campaign has displaced tens and tens of thousands of people, turning them into starving refugees.

The United Nations and some NGOs [nongovernmental organizations] relentlessly promote the theme that gun ownership is contrary to human rights. Yet the UN and the NGOs are too often silent about the extreme human rights violations that are currently being perpetrated as a result of the UN gun control campaign.

United Nations gun control is the cause of a massive humanitarian crisis in East Africa. Any new United Nations Programme of Action [to Prevent, Combat and Eradicate the Illicit Trade in Small Arms and Light Weapons in All Its Aspects] ... should include concrete measures to ensure that UN gun control does not lead directly to rape, pillage, murder, and de facto ethnic cleansing.

Kenyan Gun Control Laws

Prasad Kariyawasam, the Sri Lankan chair of the UN conference, says that the conference "does not in any way address legal possession." The statement is meant to be reassuring to American gun owners, but, in practice, the statement simply means that gun confiscation will be implemented once the UN has succeeded in getting national governments to eliminate the legal ownership of firearms. For example, UNESCO [United Nations Educational, Scientific and Cultural Organization] and UNICEF [the United Nations Children's Fund] funded the supporters of the October 2005 referendum in Brazil, which would have outlawed citizen firearms possession.

In Kenya, the existence of a gun licensing program creates the legal fiction that law-abiding Kenyan citizens can possess a firearm. But in reality, "Very few Kenyan citizens, especially those living in remote areas, meet the criteria for a gun license and can afford to pay the associated fees." In the *Daily Nation*, Peter Mwaura explained, "In practice, however, only the rich and the socially or politically correct or well-connected manage to obtain firearms certificates and keep them. . . . Thus the gun law can be pretty arbitrary and subjective in its application."

Ordinary Kenyans are not even allowed to possess bows and arrows, and the bow and arrow laws are also applied discriminatorily.

Among the pastoralists of the Kenya/Uganda borderlands, many households have firearms, and the crime rate is low, although there is a substantial problem of violence between tribes and clans, especially in cattle raiding. Estimates of the pastoralists' gun stock range from 50,000 to 200,000 in Kenya, and 50,000 to 150,000 in Uganda.

Yet even the worst intertribal cattle-raiding violence is exceeded by the violence of the gun confiscation programs. According to the Kenyan newspaper the *Standard*, "Internal Security Minister Mirugi Kariuki said the government would stop at nothing to recover the arms." West Pokot area District Commissioner Stephen Ikua warned, "We shall use force to get them."

In March 2006, a shoot-to-kill directive for the entire country of Kenya was issued to police by Internal Security Minister John Michuki, giving the police free rein against the populace. "The Kenya National Commission on Human Rights cautioned Kenyans to brace themselves for a killing field if police officers were to effect the order."

Previous Gun Prohibition Efforts

Extreme brutality in the enforcement of gun prohibition is nothing new in Kenya. A gun confiscation program that the military conducted in 1950 caused the deaths of 50 people, while the government confiscated 10,000 head of cattle.

In 1961, then Lieutenant Colonel Idi Amin of the King's African Rifles in the then British colony of Uganda crossed the border into Kenya and tortured and terrorized members of the Turkana tribe who refused to give up their weapons. At least 127 men were castrated and left to die.

The failed 1984 "Operation NYUNDO" [Operation Hammer] was a brutal example of the difficulty of disarming civilians who would rather risk death than surrender their ability to protect their families. "Operation NYUNDO" was a collaborative effort of the Kenyan and Ugandan armies—as are the current gun confiscation programs in those countries.

Krop Muroto, a political activist, recalled: "No one knows to date how many people were killed in that operation that lasted three months. The community was further devastated by mass killing of their cattle. 20,000 head of cattle were confiscated, rounded up in sheds and starved to death. Among other atrocities ... the army used helicopter gunships, killed people and destroyed a lot of property."

A May 11, 2006, article by Reuters reported:

"Lopokoy Kolimuk, an elder in the dusty and dry village of Kanyarkwat in the West Pokot district, said the soldiers who carried out that mission were 'wild, beyond humanity.'" He said many shot Pokots on sight, or forced men to lie on the ground in a line as they ran across their backs. Other men had their testicles tied together and were then made to run away from each other, he said. Women were raped in front of their husbands, sometimes with empty beer bottles."

The atrocities in 1950, 1961, and 1984 were not committed as part of a United Nations program. Surely the contemporary gun confiscation program, being conducted at the wishes of the United Nations, would show respect for human rights?

"Fearing a repeat of the 1984 human rights violations that accompanied disarmament, 15,000 panicked people fled to Uganda with their cattle and guns."

Current Gun Control Efforts in Kenya

To the contrary, in April 2006, [Internal] Security Minister John Michuki told Parliament, "The government has decided to disarm the Pokot by force. If they want an experience of 1984 when the government used force to disarm them, then this is precisely what is going to happen."

Stephen Ikua, a government representative, said that threats were necessary in order to get civilians to peacefully surrender their firearms. He said: "As a government, you should talk from a position of strength. You cannot come in saying you are going to respect human rights."

On May 4, 2006, the BBC described the latest military operation in Kenya, code named "Okota" [Collect], utilizing tanks, trucks, helicopters, and a local school building as barracks for the army. In the village of about 2,000 people, eight weapons were recovered by the intimidation. Fearing a repeat of the 1984 human rights violations that accompanied disarmament, 15,000 panicked people fled to Uganda with their cattle and guns, leaving behind the aged, infirm, and the children.

The *Standard* reported on May 18:

"Starvation and anguish are now stalking West Pokot residents, since the government launched a forcible disarmament exercise a month ago. . . . The residents now say they have resigned themselves to fate and have become refugees in their own country. . . . A recent visit by the *Standard* revealed the sense of hopelessness and vulnerability that the disarmament has brought, forcing majority residents to relocate to Uganda. Schools have also become ghost institutions, with very few pupils. . . . Although the government says the operation has not disrupted the villagers' normal life, a spot-check reveals otherwise."

In West Pokot alone, 120,000 people need food aid, but only half are getting rations. Schooling is disrupted, and farmsteads are being neglected.

Five weeks after the forced disarmament program began, 70 illegally possessed firearms had been recovered. Apparently, a few dozen firearms are reason enough for the Kenyan government to go to war against its own citizenry.

Gun Confiscation Programs in Uganda

In 1970, Uganda's Firearms Act imposed national firearm registration and gun-owner licensing under exceedingly stringent requirements. In practice, the law was used to make it illegal for anyone to have a firearm, except persons deemed politically correct by the dictatorship of Milton Obote.

A year later, Army Chief of Staff Idi Amin wrested control of the country in a military coup. The ensuing genocide of the Amin regime was perpetrated against a populace whose primitive armaments did not approach the effectiveness of the killer government. By the time the genocide ended in 1979, the estimated toll was 300,000 slaughtered Ugandans, the Karamojong tribespeople suffering a disproportionately higher percentage at about 30,000 tribespersons.

In response to Amin's murderous rule, the Karamojong began fabricating their own guns, fashioning gun barrels from the steel tubing of metal furniture. These homemade guns were then used tactically to acquire better and more powerful ones by attacking isolated police outposts where acquisition would not be terribly costly in terms of tribal lives. When the Amin government was toppled and his army fled, military firearms were traded, sold, or lost along the way to local tribesmen, who also found easy access to now-deserted weapons depots.

Obote was restored to power in 1979, after Amin attacked Tanzania, and was toppled by the Tanzanian army. Obote again began to attempt to disarm the Karamojong. His efforts were forcefully repelled. The Karamojong had learned that cows and guns are equally indispensable: A person needs a gun immediately at hand to protect one's herd. The most-armed tribes fared the best.

Defeating Obote and seizing power in 1986, President Yoweri Museveni reconstituted his rebel forces as the new national army. Like his predecessors, Museveni attempted to subdue the Karamojong. In *Africa Studies Quarterly*, Michael Quam explains that "the soldiers misbehaved, bullying people and looting stores, and generally convincing the Karamojong that their only protection from men with guns lay in keeping guns themselves." The Ugandan government's coercive disarmament efforts met with so much resistance that Museveni let the matter drop in 1989.

But Museveni started a new gun confiscation program at the behest of the United Nations. When a voluntary gun surrender program expired in Uganda on February 15, 2002, and only a disappointing 7,676 guns were collected, President Museveni turned up the heat. The UN Integrated Regional Information Networks [IRIN] announced that "the forcible disarmament operation will involve the use of 'police methods'...." What the UN delicately called "police methods" might more precisely be termed "Gestapo methods."

The UPDF (the Ugandan army, or Uganda People's Defence Forces) rampaged, beating and torturing Ugandans, and raping and looting at will, all the while using firearm confiscation to justify the violence.

On March 21, 2002, Father Declan O'Toole, a member of the Mill Hill Missionaries in Uganda, and his companions were executed by UPDF soldiers because O'Toole asked the army to be "less aggressive" in the disarmament campaign. The murderers were apprehended and their death sentence was carried out within days, before they could appeal it—and also before they could reveal who had given them the order. Just one week after O'Toole's murder, New Vision reported the death of an expectant mother who "died of injuries sustained when a soldier kicked her in the stomach during forceful disarmament." The article also noted the "complaints of torturing civilians by the UPDF."

Museveni's answer was to blame the victim Karamojong, whose torture by the army was the basis for O'Toole's complaint. Museveni "said the best way to stop such incidents in [the] future is for the Karamojong to hand in their guns to eliminate any justification for the UPDF operations in the villages."

The Mandera Triangle Disarmament

The joint police-military disarmament operation in the Mandera Triangle [in Kenya] began on October 25, 2008. It was ostensibly an attempt to address one of the underlying causes of insecurity in the region by seizing illegal firearms from warring Garre and Murulle communities. For the next few days around 600 personnel from the regular Kenyan police, Administration Police, and Kenyan army targeted Garre and Murulle settlements in the districts of Mandera Central and Mandera East. The approach was simple: Security forces terrorized the civilian population through violence while demanding that they turn over illegal weapons if they wanted the violence to stop. By the time the operation was over on October 28, more than 1,200 people from both clans were injured as a result of severe beatings and torture by the security forces; one person died. The government hailed the operation as a success because it claimed to have seized 130 illegal firearms and arrested more than 150 Ethiopian and Somali militiamen found on Kenyan soil and implicated in the clashes that triggered the operation.

Human Rights Watch,
Bring the Guns or You'll Die, *June 29, 2009.*
www.hrw.org.

The Fallout of Forcible Disarmament

By May 2002, reports of fierce resistance from the remaining armed Karamojong began to trickle out, despite government attempts to suppress knowledge of that resistance and of the army's brutality. For example, in Kotido, on May 16, the Ugandan army engaged armed civilians and recovered about 30 rifles. Thirteen civilians and two soldiers died, an average of one death for each two guns confiscated.

"After many homes were bombed and crops were destroyed, tribesmen fled across the border to Kenya. About 80,000 people were internally displaced." The Catholic Church charged that thousands of residents of Karamoja were turned into refugees after their homes were torched by UPDF troops in the disarmament campaign. By mid-July, the total number of confiscated guns had reached 10,000—only about 25 percent of the expected total.

Disarmed civilians were preyed upon by those who still had weapons. Kenyans who had credulously surrendered their guns were not rewarded with tranquility, but instead found themselves especially vulnerable. As New Vision had earlier reported, "Most of the people whose cows were taken" in a raid in the recently disarmed Bokora district, "had handed in their guns to the government in the ongoing disarmament exercise."

In May 2006, at least nine more civilians and three soldiers were killed in "forceful disarmament" operations that seized a few dozen guns. Nongovernmental organizations that support voluntary Ugandan disarmament, have, speaking anonymously, called the army's forcible program "very cruel," because of its "endangering the lives of people."

Ben Knighton, presenting a paper at an Oxford University conference, reported a damning list of human rights abuses that constitute the disarmament program. He commented: "Without guns any Karamojong is at the mercy of brutal soldiers. . . . The state is just another raider."

Knighton charged that the violence was "due to an escalation in raiding directly stimulated by a disarmament programme," and that even that degree of violence among the pastoralists may be overstated by gun prohibition activists and the Ugandan government. He noted that, in Karamoja, although there is a lack of medical reporting, making precise figures unavailable: "With 130 gunshot wounds being treated a year in both the main hospitals (0.35 [wounds] per thousand), it is small beer compared with 22,000 murders in South Africa in 2000 (0.51 [deaths] per thousand). This analysis is directly counter to alarmist international aid views, 'the source of modern violence in Karamoja is automatic weaponry.'"

In sum, Knighton warns that if the Ugandan forced disarmament program "succeeds it will accomplish the ethnocide of the nomadic pastoralist culture . . . if not their genocide."

The First Step to Reform

On June 28, 2006, the *Washington Post* published an Associated Press report that the UN Development Programme (UNDP) had sent a letter to the Ugandan government on June 26, announcing the halt of UN financial assistance for the disarmament program in Karamoja. The letter noted the "killings, beatings, arbitrary detention, intimidation and harassment" perpetrated by Ugandan "security" forces.

The UN's action is laudable, and should be applauded by all human rights supporters. This is the first time that the United Nations has ever criticized human rights abuses in a disarmament program. It would have been better, of course, if the entire international community had taken much stronger action starting in 2002, when it became clear what the Ugandan army was doing in Karamoja. Instead, tens of thousands of Ugandans were turned into refugees, their villages burned, and their livelihood destroyed by the disarmament program.

Thus far, the United Nations has remained silent about the similar human rights abuses being perpetrated by Kenya's disarmament program.

Predictably, the Ugandan government's speech to the UN gun control conference did not even mention the UNDP letter, and offered no indication that Uganda would make any changes in its program of ethnocide by disarmament.

While this [viewpoint] has focused on Kenya and Uganda, they are not the only nations where disarmament has directly led to the violations of international human rights. Guns in the wrong hands are a global problem, and so are human rights violations caused by forced disarmament in nations such as Zimbabwe, Bougainville, Cambodia, and Albania— and perhaps many others, where suppression of the free press has prevented the world from learning the full scope of other human rights abuses.

Small Arms Transfers

Quite clearly, the leading source of modern violence and human rights violations in the Kenya-Uganda border is the gun confiscation program.

Speaking to the United Nations small arms conference on June 27, 2006, Cyrus T. Gituai, Permanent Secretary, Provincial Administration/Internal Security, Office of the President of Kenya, claimed that arms "transfers fanned violence, eroded human development and seriously undermined peace efforts."

"Quite clearly, the leading source of modern violence and human rights violations in the Kenya-Uganda border is the gun confiscation program."

In truth, it is the arms "transfers" (that is, confiscations) perpetrated by the Kenyan and Ugandan governments, and the arms that other nations have transferred to the abusive Kenyan and Ugandan militaries that are fanning violence, eroding development, and destroying the peace.

Both Kenyan and Ugandan governments state that their gun confiscation programs are carrying out the wishes of the United Nations, pursuant to the Nairobi Protocol, an East African treaty banning unlicensed gun possession (in practice, banning all gun possession by anyone except the ruling elites). The Nairobi Protocol is a result of the UN's "Programme of Action" from the previous major UN conference on gun control, in 2001.

IANSA (International Action Network on Small Arms) is the world's leading international gun prohibition group; its staff members are serving as delegates for some nations at the 2006 gun control conference, and one of its members, professor Barbara Frey, is the UN's Special Rapporteur on guns and human rights. The organization has been inappropriately reticent about the Kenya and Uganda atrocities, praising the governmental actions with the euphemism of "forced disarmament."

Many human rights activists correctly point out that guns in the wrong hands can be used to violate human rights, such as the guns possessed by the genocidal Janjaweed Arab tribal gangsters in Darfur, which are armed and supported by the Government of Sudan, or the terrorist Lord's Resistance Army in Sudan and Uganda. Similarly, the guns in the hands of the Kenyan and Ugandan governments are a major cause of human rights abuses today in the Kenya-Uganda borderlands.

"As a result, disarmament campaigns would generally be voluntary—supported by public education and financial rewards—and would not be coercive."

The Only Humanitarian Solution

The proper program of action is clear for human rights activists whose top priority is human rights (as opposed to self-proclaimed "human rights" supporters whose real priority is gun confiscation regardless of human rights): Genuine human rights activists should work to ensure that all disarmament campaigns, especially those undertaken pursuant to UN efforts, meet the same high standards of adherence of human rights as would be expected of any other government campaign.

As a result, disarmament campaigns would generally be voluntary—supported by public education and financial rewards—and would not be coercive.

[Julius] Arile Lomerinyang, a former tribal warrior in Kenya, traveled to New York City to present a gun control petition. Yet even he rejects what the Kenyan government is doing. According to the *East African*, "he says the Kenya government is going about the whole [disarmament] exercise the wrong way. 'It won't yield any fruit. Local residents, especially the Pokots, were never consulted. The government assumed the big-boss mentality by not inviting our leaders for any discussions.'" . . .

"He went further to accuse the government of using excessive force and acting at the behest of foreigners. He claims some residents have fled to Uganda to escape the forced disarmament. Those left behind have hidden their firearms. 'Very few weapons, if any, will be recovered. It is an exercise in futility.'"

Supporters of human rights can have legitimate disagreements about the circumstances when disarmament will genuinely advance human rights. But no sincere advocate of human rights can dispute that the Kenya/Uganda program of "forced disarmament" is a massive human rights atrocity, an evil program that must be condemned by the international community just as forcefully as any other government program that produces so much cruelty—wanton murder, rape, torture, arson, and turning so many innocent men, women, and children into starving refugees.

Periodical Bibliography

The following articles have been selected to supplement the diverse views presented in this chapter.

Ian Austen   "Canada Debates Gun Control, and Ideals; Debating Gun Control, and Ideals, in Canada; Shotgun-and-Rifle Registry Heads Toward Elimination Amid an Emotional Fight," *International Herald Tribune*, December 8, 2009.

Maria de Fátima Marinho de Souza et al.   "Reductions in Firearm-Related Mortality and Hospitalizations in Brazil After Gun Control," *Health Affairs*, vol. 26, no. 2, March/April 2007.

Tom Diaz   "Guns, Gun Control, and American Jews," *Sh'ma: A Journal of Jewish Responsibility*, November 3, 2009.

Don B. Kates and Gary Mauser   "Would Banning Firearms Reduce Murder and Suicide?" *Harvard Journal of Law and Public Policy*, vol. 30, no. 2, Spring 2007.

David B. Kopel, Carlisle E. Moody, and Howard Nemerov   "Is There a Relationship Between Guns and Freedom? Comparative Results from Fifty-Nine Nations," *Texas Review of Law and Politics*, vol. 13, no. 1, Fall 2008.

Medical Ethics Advisor   "Gun Control: Medical Ethics Issue, Public Health Concern, or Political Bias?" June 2007.

A. Lin Neumann   "The Insanity of America's Gun Culture," *Asia Sentinel*, April 18, 2007.

Carolyn E. Snider, Howard Ovens, Alan Drummond, and Atul K. Kapur   "CAEP Position Statement on Gun Control," *CJEM: Canadian Journal of Emergency Medicine*, vol. 11, no. 1, January 2009.

John Stossel   "Gun Control Puts People at Risk," *Human Events*, March 10, 2008.

The Impact of the Global Arms Trade

The Global Trade in Small Arms Must Be Regulated

Integrated Regional Information Networks (IRIN)

Integrated Regional Information Networks (IRIN), a project of the United Nations Office for the Coordination of Humanitarian Affairs, provides news and analysis about sub-Saharan Africa, the Middle East, and parts of Asia for the humanitarian community. In the following viewpoint, IRIN describes the direct and indirect results of guns as rationale for the development of a strong set of guidelines that would limit the production and trade of small arms around the world. Although much progress has been made, IRIN argues that global laws must be passed for the well-being of all the world's citizens.

As you read, consider the following questions:

1. What portion of the global arms trade constitutes small arms?

2. What percentage of small arms traded on the black market originates in state-sanctioned trade?

3. Of the three hundred thousand people shot each year worldwide, how many are killed in gun-related homicides?

A re small arms, as many describe them, the real weapons of mass destruction? Easily available and simple to use, small arms are the instruments of modern violence. The global trade in these weapons is scarcely regulated, and continues to fuel both armed conflict and violent crime. Until transfers of small arms are controlled, and limited, the human costs and the implications for long-term development will continue to be devastating.

Small arms have a disproportionate impact—while accounting for only one-fifth of the global arms trade, they maim and kill far more than any other conventional weapons. Small arms were the most commonly used weapons—and in some instances the only weapons—used in the 101 conflicts fought worldwide between 1989 and 1996. They are relatively inexpensive, portable and easy to use, and are effortlessly recycled from one conflict or violent community to the next. Their durability perpetuates their lethality. An assault rifle, for example, can be operational for 20 to 40 years with little maintenance.

All agencies involved in the fight against small arms agree that now is a critical time to curtail the further proliferation of small arms. A study commissioned by the United Nations World Health Organization [WHO] and the World Bank found that by 2020, the number of deaths and injuries resulting from war and violence would overtake the number of deaths caused by diseases such as measles and malaria. In addition, 2006 is a significant year with respect to efforts to control the global trade in small arms. A major UN [United Nations] conference to review the organisation's process on small arms will take place in July, and it is possible a resolution will be proposed in the UN General Assembly First Committee on Disarmament and [International] Security in October to begin negotiations for an arms trade treaty. Perhaps the catalogue of despair associated with small arms will begin to be addressed on the world stage....

An Absence of Global Standards

There are currently no universally accepted, legally binding global standards that apply in every country to prevent irresponsible arms transfers. The duty to control small-arms transfers ultimately lies with governments, demanding both the will and capacity to act at the government level if effective legislation is to be enacted. National-level export regimes are often flawed by legislative loopholes that permit the transfer of small arms to irresponsible end users, or lack laws to prohibit arms brokering.

While the United Nations Programme of Action to Prevent, Combat and Eradicate the Illicit Trade in Small Arms and Light Weapons [in All Its Aspects], the result of a 2001 conference, defines measures the governments of member states should take to prevent and control black market arms transfers and brokering, it is not binding.

> *"There are currently no universally accepted, legally binding global standards that apply in every country to prevent irresponsible arms transfers."*

Equally, regional agreements covering the licensed arms trade, such as the European Union [EU] Code of Conduct on Arms Exports, only give recommendations to governments. The EU Code of Conduct may suggest admirable criteria for signatories to consider when granting export licenses to arms manufacturers, but it has failed to prevent certain transfers that resulted in gross human rights abuses. Asking governments to notify all other members of license denials certainly does not ensure notification; particularly as such nonbinding agreements can be interpreted differently by participants.

Such agreements are further weakened by omissions. The UN Programme of Action fails to address the licensed arms trade in any form, while regional agreements often address only specific aspects of the arms trade. In addition, existing regional and international agreements only request that governments act to curb future arms transfers, proposing little regarding the control of arms already in circulation. By focusing on simply controlling the supply of arms, these agreements also fail to recognise the significance of demand—as long as there is demand, arms production will continue, and, in the absence of stringent, universal controls, many of these arms will inevitably find themselves in the wrong hands. A critical aspect of controlling the illicit arms trade must therefore be the eradication, or at least the reduction, of demand.

Legislative Failure at the National Level

Without being legally bound by international agreements to control the trade in small arms, states by and large have demonstrated little inclination to implement effective laws.

Indeed, a 2005 independent review of progress of the UN Programme of Action, by Biting the Bullet—a joint project between International Alert, Saferworld and the University of Bradford—and the International Action Network on Small Arms (IANSA), documented a veritable absence of action by states. Laws governing arms transfers were found to be inadequate or out-of-date in many countries. The review noted that more than 100 states have failed to enact what is considered to be a minimum step towards implementation—that is, establishing governmental bodies to coordinate action on small arms at a national level—while more than 120 countries have failed even to review their laws and regulations on small arms.

In instances where there are more comprehensive export-control regimes, legislative loopholes undermine their efficacy. By licensing production to another country—that is, outsourcing production, often to the purchasing country—labour costs are lowered and controls over arms transfers that may apply in some countries can be evaded. Research by the Omega Foundation suggested that companies in at least 15 countries, including the US, United Kingdom, Russia, France, Germany and Switzerland, have established agreements permitting the production of arms in 45 other countries.

In addition, major producers have repeatedly shown a disregard for UN arms embargoes, continuing to export to countries plagued by conflict and insecurity. According to the Control Arms Campaign, a global partnership between Amnesty International, Oxfam [International] and IANSA, every one of the 13 embargoes imposed by the UN in the last 10 years has been repeatedly violated, with very few of the embargo breakers named in UN sanctions reports successfully prosecuted.

Arms embargoes are also rarely applied. The Stockholm International Peace Research Institute (SIPRI) found that between 1990 and 2001, there were 57 separate major armed conflicts, with only eight of them subject to UN arms embargoes. "Such embargoes are usually late and blunt instruments, and the UN sanctions committees, which oversee the embargoes, have to rely largely on member states to monitor and implement them," SIPRI said. "Therefore, arms embargoes cannot be deployed effectively as an instrument by the UN to prevent illicit arms trafficking, without better national controls on international arms transfers. These controls are woefully inadequate."

"While the value of the black market trade in small arms may be relatively small-scale . . . it is almost impossible to control."

Diversion into the Black Market

Not only does the legal trade in small arms sometimes directly supply irresponsible end users, the absence of controls means guns can easily be diverted into the black market. Estimates suggest that 80 percent to 90 percent of the small arms traded on the black market originate in state-sanctioned trade.

While the value of the black market trade in small arms may be relatively small-scale—worth around $1 billion—it is almost impossible to control. In addition, the durability of small arms means they can easily be recycled from one conflict to another, or passed between the hands of different criminals. The recent conflicts in West Africa are but one arresting example of this, with guns passing from, and continuing to wreak devastation in, Sierra Leone to Liberia, and now most recently to Côte d'Ivoire.

Small arms move into the illegal arena in various ways. Governments at war, for example, may transfer weapons to sympathetic non-state actors. Security forces and other authorised weapons users may supply and sell arms, while civilians, aided by inadequate regulation, can purchase firearms and then illegally sell them on, in a process known as the 'ant trade'.

Weapons may be purchased or stolen from poorly guarded government stockpiles, or recovered from the battlefield following combat. In 2002, for example, arms collected in Albania were transferred to Rwanda, from where they were allegedly passed on to eastern Democratic Republic of [the] Congo (DRC). In addition, disarmament programmes or changes of weaponry by armed forces can flood the black market with weapons, as was the case after former Warsaw Pact countries sold off the standard arms they had been using.

Arms brokers—effectively middlemen—also play a key role, and have been implicated in supplying some of the worst conflict zones and areas most notorious for human rights abuses, including Afghanistan, Angola, the DRC, Iraq, Rwanda, Sierra Leone and South Africa. As the arrangement of arms deals is an unregulated area, arms brokers can operate outside the law and traffic arms illegally on behalf of governments or private actors. Even where controls do exist at the national level—fewer than 40 countries were found in 2005 to have them—brokers either rely on a lack of political will to enforce such laws or simply move offshore.

Arms embargoes are also no barrier. Brokers find ways of either avoiding controls or colluding with authorities. Creating a complex supply chain involving many front companies and handling agents, using fraudulent or misleading paperwork, and routing deliveries through third countries that may not be subject to embargo restrictions are just some of the tactics deployed by brokers.

Progress—but Not Enough

Although the global trade in small arms may ultimately be unregulated, it is important to acknowledge the significant progress of recent years in establishing instruments and processes at the international, regional and national levels. The Control Arms Campaign has worked extensively to bring the issue to the fore.

The UN process on small arms was launched with the first international conference on small arms in July 2001, which produced the aforementioned UN Programme of Action. While the document has been criticised for neglecting various key issues, notably those of civilian possession, transfers to non-state actors and the misuse of arms by state forces, it served to put small arms on the agenda for many states. A final review conference on the effectiveness of this process is due in July of this year, following two biennial conferences in 2003 and 2005.

Also in 2003, Barbara Frey was appointed UN Special Rapporteur on the prevention of human rights violations committed with small arms and light weapons. According to Frey, "Small arms have a pervasive impact on human rights, and it is thus of vital importance to highlight this impact and to outline what legal obligations states may have to take steps against such abuses."

Small Arms = Big Business

Making and selling small arms is a worldwide business. Nearly 7 million commercial handguns and long guns are produced annually. About 75% of these are made in the USA or the European Union. Other important producers include Brazil, China, Canada, Japan and the Russian Federation.

- At least 90 countries can or do produce small arms and/or ammunition.

- Around 16 billion units of ammunition were produced during 2001.

- The value of small arms and ammunition production was at least US$7.4 billion in 2000.

- The global small arms stockpile is estimated at 639 million guns. Approximately 59% of this arsenal is in the hands of civilians—over 377 million weapons. The remainder [is] owned by government armed forces (about 39%), police, insurgents and other non-state forces.

IANSA, "Small Arms Are Weapons of Mass Destruction," 1999–2006. www.iansa.org.

In 2001, the UN also agreed on the Firearms Protocol, the first legally binding international agreement on small arms, amongst other things criminalising the illicit trafficking of firearms. It fails, however, to address some key issues or establish criteria to govern transfers, and only 49 states have signed and ratified the protocol.

A growing number of regional agreements have also been concluded, demonstrating the importance of regional cooperation, especially where borders are porous. While many are neither binding nor comprehensive, some go much further than the UN Programme of Action and are legally binding. This is true of the Southern African Development Community [SADC] Protocol and the Nairobi Protocol, which covers the Great Lakes region and the Horn of Africa. These also totally prohibit civilian possession and the use of all light weapons.

"While all of these developments are steps in the right direction, the trade in small arms is unrelenting, and human costs are as patent as ever."

As discussed, legislation on small arms has been enacted in many countries. However, there [are] relatively few countries with effective legislation, and global standards are ultimately vital. If neighbouring countries have weaker legislation, guns may simply leak across the border.

While all of these developments are steps in the right direction, the trade in small arms is unrelenting, and human costs are as patent as ever. . . .

Direct Casualties

The Small Arms Survey estimated that 300,000 people are shot dead over the course of a year. Gun homicides account for around 200,000 of these deaths, the majority occurring in Latin America and the Caribbean, while 60,000 to 90,000 people are killed by small arms in conflict settings. In many contemporary conflicts, civilian deaths outnumber those of combatants.

Approximately 50,000 more deaths result from gun suicides. Over one million people are believed to suffer firearms-related injuries on an annual basis. While the accuracy of these figures can never be guaranteed, given that much data is inevitably incomplete, the magnitude is sobering.

While men are the primary perpetrators, and indeed victims, of armed violence, vulnerable groups are often disproportionately affected. Women and children are killed and injured in great numbers. Many are victims of sexual violence committed at gunpoint, and they usually constitute a large number of those forcibly displaced by armed violence. Gender is a critical factor in determining the nature of the impact of armed violence. . . .

Indirect Deaths

Indirect deaths, in addition to tangible fatal and nonfatal injuries, are a critical human cost of small arms. Although ultimately unquantifiable, indirect deaths represent those who did not die from a bullet wound, but as a result of circumstances caused by armed violence. Be it through starvation or the withdrawal of aid, such excess mortality cannot, of course, be pinned wholly on firearms. However, despite many other influential factors, the consequences of armed violence, and conflict in particular, are severe and lasting.

"We have typically looked at the body count when assessing the impact of weapons, but it is misleading to look only at the direct deaths," said Debbie Hillier of Oxfam. "In the conflict in the Democratic Republic of [the] Congo, for example, large numbers of people have been killed directly, either in combat or in the cross fire. However, 95 percent of the deaths were caused not by bullets, but by malnutrition or preventable diseases such as malaria, which were contracted when people were forced out of their homes by the conflict."

A gun may not ostensibly be culpable for the death of a malnourished child. This child, however, may have been forced to leave his home at gunpoint in a time of war, to flee from productive land and a nearby clinic to a locale so militarised that even the most hardened aid agencies have given up attempting to supply food and medical aid. The ultimate cause of death may be starvation, but the chaos and destruction perpetrated at the barrel of a gun lay the foundation of this tragic end, illustrating the indirect, destructive impact of guns in unregulated settings.

In countries at peace, the indirect effects of gun violence are also significant, if less multifarious. Victims and witnesses of such violence experience a decline in physical and mental health, resulting in inflated costs for society in terms of treatment for firearm-related injury and lost productivity through disability or premature death. A survey in the US estimated the annual cost of gun violence to be $80 million. While countries such as the US may be able to absorb such extra outlay relatively easily, the cost of armed violence of any form has serious implications for the long-term development prospects of more marginalised countries.

"It is clear that the gun business is simply not worth enough money to make tolerating gun violence worthwhile," said IANSA's Rebecca Peters. "A member of IANSA in El Salvador has calculated that the extra annual costs associated with dealing with gunshot injuries would equal the cost of a brand new hospital. . . . The sums just do not add up." . . .

A Time to Act

These multifarious, and generally devastating, effects of the unregulated proliferation of small arms highlight the urgency with which action must be taken. This need for action echoes the calls that have been made again and again in the past decade by both mainstream and specialist international NGOs [nongovernmental organisations], various UN agencies, individual activists and some states.

While progress has been made in recent years at the national, regional and international levels, global and universal standards, to which all countries are bound, are still needed. The call for such standards—to cover both legal and illegal transfers as well as control the brokering, licensing and transit of small arms—is part of the core recommendations from agencies working to address the problem. Although there will always be a demand for weapons, effective control of the trade would significantly curtail the supply of guns, which is an important first step.

The Passage of a Global Arms Trade Treaty Is Essential

Brian Wood

In the following viewpoint, Brian Wood, Amnesty International's arms control manager, argues that passing a global arms trade treaty is essential for the well-being of all the world's nations. Despite attempts by the United Nations, many countries across the globe, including the United States, China, and Russia, have blocked the passage of such a treaty. These countries outwardly express concern about the impact it would have on their citizens' freedoms, but Wood argues that they are resistant because of the money they make for exporting small arms.

As you read, consider the following questions:

1. Which eight countries make up the Group of Eight (G8)?
2. Which groups of people make up most refugees?
3. What happened in Andizhan in May 2005?

The world's governments meet in New York at the end of [June 2006] to discuss how to enhance the United Nations [UN] Programme of Action [to Prevent, Combat and Eradicate the Illicit Trade in] Small Arms and Light Weapons [in All Its Aspects]. So far the programme has not considered

Brian Wood, "A Dirty Trade in Arms," *Le Monde Diplomatique*, June 2006, pp. 1–4. Copyright © 1997–2008 *Le Monde Diplomatique*. This article reprinted from *Le Monde Diplomatique*'s English language version, available online at www.mondediplo.com. Reproduced by permission.

respect for human rights, although the UN charter refers to this duty; the programme also leaves crucial aspects of arms control, such as rules for international transfers, almost untouched. The conference will be confrontational for those who want better global security.

Approaches to the global small arms problem first emerged after terrible conflicts in Africa and the Balkans in the 1990s, including genocide in Rwanda. A growing global campaign demands tough control and will not disappear (especially now that it has some government support). But an alliance of the United States [US], China, Russia and some non-aligned states threatens to block any significant conference moves to tighten controls.

The trade in small arms and light weapons is only a fraction of that in conventional military equipment, but is just as lethal. Secrecy and lack of accountability mean that accurate, up-to-date statistics on the global arms trade are hard to obtain and must be treated with caution. However, one set of data, based on estimates of military articles and services traded by value, claims that 35 countries are responsible for 90% of the world's arms exports, and that, during the period 1997–2005, developing countries' share of such imports increased to 68.5%.

Seven of the world's top arms exporters—Canada, France, Germany, Italy, Japan (whose exports are relatively small), Russia, the US and Britain—belong to the Group of Eight (G8). Amnesty International (AI), Oxfam International and the International Action Network on Small Arms (IANSA), acting together in the Control Arms Campaign, published a report in June 2005 revealing how these countries supplied equipment, weapons and munitions to destinations where they contribute to violations of human rights. Loopholes and weaknesses in arms export controls across G8 countries undermine their commitments to poverty reduction, stability and human rights; irresponsible exports by some G8 countries went to such poor and conflict-ridden countries as Sudan, Myanmar (Burma), the Democratic Republic of [the] Congo (DRC), Colombia and the Philippines. Arms transfers by these major powers are supplemented by exports from China and medium-sized, arms-producing states such as Brazil, Israel, the Netherlands, Singapore, North Korea, South Africa, all competing for markets.

"The trade in small arms and light weapons is only a fraction of that in conventional military equipment, but is just as lethal."

If an importer cannot get what it wants directly, it will shop around and may buy indirectly. In June 2005 AI called on the governments of India, Britain, the US, Belgium, Germany, South Africa and France to suspend all military and security-related transfers to Nepal until its government halted human rights violations and brought those responsible to justice. When India, the US and Britain temporarily suspended supplies in 2004, the Nepalese government secured arms from China, covert supplies from the US government and offers of more from Pakistan. Among the purchases from India had been helicopters assembled from French parts.

The Role of Brokers

A key aspect of global competition to sell arms is the role of brokers, who often work in networks with transport and financial agents. Only about 35 states have laws regulating them, so they collaborate with government officials to supply cheap weaponry to rulers and warlords. In July 2005 an AI report showed that large quantities of weapons and ammunition from the Balkans and Eastern Europe were flowing into Africa's Great Lakes region, although it was known that they led to human rights violations. The shipments continued to the Democratic Republic of [the] Congo despite a peace process initiated in 2002 and a UN arms embargo. AI revealed the role played by arms dealers, brokers and transporters from Albania, Bosnia [and] Herzegovina, Croatia, the Czech Republic, Israel, Russia, Serbia, South Africa, Britain and the US; it traced the supply to the governments of the DRC, Rwanda and Uganda and its distribution to armed groups and militia in eastern DRC that were involved in war crimes and crimes against humanity.

The proliferation of arms, especially small arms, has had a lasting impact on human rights. In the Mano River states of West Africa, AI has repeatedly appealed for measures to halt arms flows that result in human rights abuses in Sierra Leone and Liberia. In October 2005 AI made public its concerns about reports of small arms proliferation, recirculation and new transfers to both sides in Ivory Coast [Côte d'Ivoire], despite the embargo imposed by the UN in November 2004. Easy access to small arms undermined the disarmament, demobilisation and reintegration processes, and contributed to violations of the cease-fire, interethnic conflict and the use of child soldiers.

Women pay a disproportionate price for the unregulated trade in small arms, in their homes and communities, during and after conflict. AI, Oxfam and IANSA have appealed to governments to address inadequate firearms regulations, poor law enforcement and widespread discrimination which worsen women's vulnerability to domestic violence and rape. In some countries, there is a murder of a woman every few hours by her partner or former partner, and the presence of a gun in the household increases the risk. Women subject to armed violence at home often get no help from the police. An increase in armed gangs glamorises gun culture and macho behaviour, increases sexual assaults on women and restricts their daily lives because of intimidation. The threat is greater during and after armed conflict: Most displaced people or refugees are women and children.

In Haiti, illegal armed groups and former military use small arms to kidnap, sexually abuse and kill with impunity. Without disarmament and justice for the victims, Haiti will sink further into crisis. In parts of the country where state authority is frail, armed groups and individuals illegally control territory and population and commit crimes without being challenged by police and other authorities.

"Women pay a disproportionate price for the unregulated trade in small arms, in their homes and communities, during and after conflict."

For millions of Brazilians who live in favelas [shantytowns], armed violence is part of daily life. They are caught between drug gangs, police and vigilante death squads in parts of cities where the rule of law does not apply. A policy of military-style incursions into favelas has failed to curb violence and has endangered the lives of some of the most vulnerable. A referendum on a total ban on the sale of guns was defeated in October 2005; many analysts have attributed that to people's despair about public security and lack of faith in the ability of the police to protect them. Nevertheless some policing projects have been successful: Diadema, a 350,000-strong community in the industrial belt of São Paulo, is an example of a well-planned, integrated social project that has reduced levels of violence.

Lack of Accountability

In many countries, the inadequate training or lack of accountability of armed police and other law enforcers has led to human rights violations. For example, Uzbek security forces indiscriminately shot into crowds in a central square in Andizhan on 12–13 May 2005, killing hundreds of civilians, and then drove armoured personnel carriers over bodies. Such indiscriminate use of force contravenes international human

"Golden Rules" for an Arms Trade Treaty

We want a global ATT [arms trade treaty] based on our "5 Golden Rules" to help stop those international transfers of conventional arms that are likely to be used for serious human rights violations, and fuel conflict and poverty.

States shall not authorise international transfers of conventional arms or ammunition where they will:

(i) be used or are likely to be used for gross violations of international human rights law or serious violations of international humanitarian law.

(ii) have an impact that would clearly undermine sustainable development or involve corrupt practices.

(iii) provoke or exacerbate armed conflict in violation of their obligations under the UN Charter and existing treaties.

(iv) contribute to an existing pattern of violent crime.

(v) risk being diverted for one of the above outcomes or for acts of terrorism.

Controlarms.org, 2003–2008.
These Golden Rules have been revised and expanded.
These Global Principles can be found in the NGO
Arms Trade Treaty Steering Committee, Position Paper No. 2,
July 2009 (http://issuu.com/controlarms/docs/
scope_types_of_weapons.english?mode=embed&layout=
http%3A%2F%2Fskin.issuu.com%2Fv%2
Flight%2Flayout.xml&showFlipBtn=true).

rights standards, including the UN Code of Conduct for Law Enforcement Officials and the UN Basic Principles on the Use of Force and Firearms by Law Enforcement Officials.

AI, Oxfam International and IANSA have expanded their Control Arms Campaign to over 100 countries. It was launched in October 2003 to help reduce arms proliferation and misuse by convincing governments to introduce tough control and an enforceable arms trade treaty based on international law. Such universal standards would save lives, prevent suffering and protect livelihoods. The campaign proposed to address the lack of a global system to track small arms and ammunition, and to hold arms traders accountable for weapons reaching human rights abusers and war criminals. A UN instrument on marking and tracing was finally agreed in 2005, but it excluded ammunition and was not legally binding.

The number of states calling for such a treaty increased in 2005 and Kenya, Finland, Costa Rica, Norway and Britain led international support. During a UN conference last July to review progress in curbing the illicit trade in small arms and light weapons under a 2001 agreement, 13 governments announced support for the Control Arms Campaign. Last October the EU [European Union] council of foreign ministers called for global support for such a treaty. By the end of 2005 about 50 governments had declared their support and the momentum was increasing; other governments, including some East African states and the Mercosur grouping of Latin American states, made statements in favour of stronger export controls based on global minimum standards.

There is support for the British position that UN negotiations on a treaty covering all conventional arms should begin in late 2006 after July's small arms conference.

Last October it was also agreed that a UN group of government experts should be set up to consider action to prevent the illicit brokering of small arms and light weapons. Some powerful and influential states, including China, Egypt and the US, are opposed to legally binding instruments to control small arms and light weapons; while states in the Middle East and Asia have as yet to be convinced to support a

strong treaty. Moreover, many governments in Africa and elsewhere do not have the capacity to implement control measures and may need expanded international assistance to deal
with the problem.

Small Arms Trade in Trinidad and Tobago Is Responsible for Increasing Crime

United Nations Office on Drugs and Crime and the Latin America and the Caribbean Region of the World Bank

In the following viewpoint, the United Nations Office on Drugs and Crime and the Latin America and the Caribbean Region of the World Bank argue that the rise in crime in the Caribbean, specifically in Trinidad and Tobago, is the result of the small arms trade. In addition, the mortality levels of victims of gun crimes have increased due to the influx of more powerful weapons. Even though firearms are not manufactured in the Caribbean, banning weapons has not proved effective. The authors assert that the world must come together to fight this growing crisis.

As you read, consider the following questions:

1. What three levels of small arms and light weapons proliferation did the CARICOM Regional Task Force on Crime and Security identify?
2. What are "straw purchasers"?
3. In Trinidad and Tobago, what percentage of the victims of fatal firearms assaults were males aged fifteen to thirty-four years?

United Nations Office on Drugs and Crime and the Latin America and the Caribbean Region of the World Bank, *Crime, Violence, and Development: Trends, Costs, and Policy Options in the Caribbean*, Washington, DC: United Nations Office on Drugs and Crime and the Latin America and the Caribbean Region of the World Bank, 2007. Reproduced by permission.

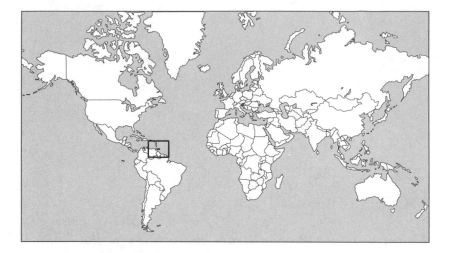

The rise of crime in the Caribbean has been characterized by the increased use of more powerful weapons, resulting in higher mortality levels. In 2004, Trinidad and Tobago experienced 160 firearm murders, 450 firearm woundings and 1,500 non-injury firearm incidents. A major factor contributing to the surge of gun-related criminality in the region is the trafficking of narcotics, which has facilitated the availability of firearms. The firearms required for protection of the contraband during transportation are smuggled in along with the drugs. Within these environments, which promote the demand for weapons, reducing gun ownership is a difficult undertaking. Better gun registries, marking and tracking can help, as can improved gun interdiction in ports. In the long term, progress will hinge on changes in the drug trade, changes in the gun culture, and progress in the implementation of international treaties and agreements on small arms and light weapons.

As violence has increased in the Caribbean, so too has the use of firearms. Increasingly, more powerful weapons are being used, resulting in higher mortality levels. The Caribbean has a long history of smuggling, and, as in the past, firearms are used in the transportation of illegal goods. "Guns and the illegal trade in drugs have formed a symbiotic relationship which has seen the emergence of increasing violence throughout the communities regionally". This [viewpoint] describes the situation in the Caribbean with respect to guns, crime, and violence. Trinidad and Tobago was selected as a case study, as it has seen a particular sharp rise in firearm-related violence over the last few years.

The CARICOM [Caribbean Community] Regional Task Force on Crime and Security recently commissioned a report on the proliferation of small arms and light weapons (SALW) in the Caribbean. The resulting report identified three levels of SALW proliferation in the region: countries with *established* high levels and patterns of armed crime (Jamaica); countries with *emerging* high levels of armed and organized criminality (Guyana, Trinidad and Tobago); and countries with *indications of increased use* and availability of small arms (Antigua and Barbuda, Barbados, Dominica, Grenada, St. Kitts and Nevis, Saint Lucia, St. Vincent and the Grenadines).

At that time, it was determined that, among CARICOM countries, only Jamaica fell in the first category, with indications that military-type weapons were available and that paramilitary units were operating. If such an evaluation were done today, Trinidad and Tobago might also be included in this tier, as the murder rate has doubled since 2002. With 160 firearm murders in 2004, these were just the tip of the iceberg with above 450 firearm woundings and 1,500 non-injury firearm incidents.

"Increasingly, more powerful weapons are being used, resulting in higher mortality levels."

For many countries of the English-speaking Caribbean, the majority of assaults and homicides were committed in past years with blunt or sharp weapons. The trend toward increased use of firearms in the commission of crime began in the 1970s in Jamaica, so that a court was established in 1974 solely dedicated to gun-related matters. In Trinidad and Tobago this change began in 2000. Before 2000, firearms were responsible for less than one-third of all homicides. By May 2006, this percentage had risen to 74 percent. The percentage of homicides attributed to firearms in Trinidad and Tobago lies well within the range of rates of 60 percent to 93 percent seen in Latin America.

The share of woundings committed with a firearm has actually decreased as the number of murders with firearms has increased. This is likely a reflection of the increasing lethality of weapons used.

Firearm Sources

There are several sources for these firearms. They may be diverted from legal owners in the country, or they may be purchased overseas (legally or illegally) and smuggled into the country. Diverted weapons come from both private owners and the protective services. In Trinidad and Tobago, authorized users of legal arms are robbed and sometimes killed for their weapons. Army and police guns go missing at intervals, and weapons that are stored at police stations for safekeeping, especially those whose owners may be deceased, are also targets for diversion to criminal use. It is believed, however, that diverted firearms are not the main source of weapons involved in crime. That role is filled by weapons smuggled into the country.

Smuggled firearms are sourced from South and Central American manufacturers of light arms, among others. Suppliers are from Brazil (which is licensed to manufacture Beretta, Colt, and Taurus makes); Venezuela (Smith & Wesson); Mexico; and the Dominican Republic. These countries all make firearms for domestic sale and for export, ostensibly to governments and licensed private owners.

Weapons manufactured or otherwise available in South America are smuggled through Venezuela, Suriname and Guyana to Trinidad and Tobago via fishing vessels and private pleasure boats. Some proceed to the United States [U.S.] and Europe, all part of the northward shipping of contraband. Weapons from the United States and Canada are transported southward in the shipping of the proceeds from the sale of illegal drugs.

"In Trinidad and Tobago, authorized users of legal arms are robbed and sometimes killed for their weapons."

Guns and other weapons are also available from disbanded guerrilla troops in post-conflict situations. Some of these are weapons that were supplied covertly two decades ago by the Cold War powers to friendly insurgents in the region. Within the Caribbean region, there is a stock of weapons surplus from previous armed conflict such as the Grenada intervention. Other countries with armed instability such as Haiti, Nicaragua and Guatemala can also be source and destination countries for the supply of illegal arms.

Another major source of firearms is the United States, the world's leading manufacturer of arms. Production, sale and exports of all arms from the United States are subject to a variety of laws and regulations, which govern the conditions under which the sales may occur and stipulate the use to which firearms may be put, even when transferred to a third party. These laws and regulations pose few or no obstacles to those wanting to buy a handgun, and unevenly enforced export regulations have made the U.S. a major supplier of illicit arms to Latin America and the Caribbean. Latin American governments report that more than half of all unlawfully acquired firearms were of U.S. origin.

One of the main strategies employed by arms traffickers to procure guns is the use of "straw purchasers." These are acquaintances, relatives or persons hired to purchase guns in the United States from gun dealers, at gun shows or directly from manufacturers. Larger orders are sometimes procured through use of counterfeit importation certificates, with the involvement of gullible or corrupt local government officials of the transit country. Trading on the knowledge that end-use checking is sloppy, these shipments are procured for an apparently legitimate use and then forwarded to a third country. Guns thus obtained become part of the stockpile of weapons available on the black market.

Finally, there are also cases of persons purchasing firearms at a gun shop in a foreign country and bringing them into the country undetected among luggage. Guns so purchased may or may not be licensed and registered for use in the destination country.

All of these guns, procured from the above-mentioned sources and by the various mechanisms, contribute to the stockpile of circulating illicit firearms. However, due to poor forensic investigation of firearm-related crimes and nonexistent tracking of firearms, it is not possible to know what contribution each of these sources makes to the problem of guns and criminality in Trinidad and Tobago.

Registration of Firearms and Seizures of Illegal Weapons

In Trinidad and Tobago, the Organised Crime, Narcotics and Firearms Bureau (OCNFB) was established in 2004. Under the Firearms Act, the Commissioner of Police is empowered to keep a national Firearms Register, although the actual existence of this database is unclear.

Seizures of firearms by the police and, more recently, the Organised Crime, Narcotics and Firearms Bureau have risen from 132 in 2000 to 199 in 2005. It is not clear whether this increase is due to increased enforcement efforts or to a greater supply of illegal weapons.

Murders Committed in Trinidad and Tobago Using a Firearm, 2001–2006

Year	Number of Murders Committed with Firearms	Total Number of Murders	Percent Murders Committed with Firearms
2001	82	151	54 percent
2002	102	172	59 percent
2003	158	229	69 percent
2004	182	259	70 percent
2005	273	386	71 percent
Jan–May 2006	123	166	74 percent

TAKEN FROM: United Nations Office on Drugs and Crime and the Latin American and the Caribbean Region of the World Bank, *Crime, Violence, and Development: Trends, Costs, and Policy Options in the Caribbean,* March 2007.

The vast majority of the weapons seized are the 9 mm pistols and .38 revolvers commonly used by criminal groups everywhere. Military weapons are rare. The seized weapons are disposed of according to the direction of the magistrate presiding over the case. They may be returned to circulation either as additions to the police armory or auctioned. This adds to the fluidity of the legal status of weapons and makes the need for identification and tracking even more critical. . . .

"The vast majority of the weapons seized are the 9 mm pistols and .38 revolvers commonly used by criminal groups everywhere."

Victims, Perpetrators, and Their Environment

Across the region, certain characteristics are common to both perpetrators and victims in gun violence. Research conducted in Latin America and the Caribbean shows that the majority of victims and perpetrators of violence are young men of low socioeconomic status, with a low level of education and poor prospects for income generation, who have witnessed violence at close range. These findings are consistent with those from a study that showed the effects of socioeconomic status, educational levels, family functioning and exposure to violence on levels of aggression and delinquency in Jamaican children. In Trinidad and Tobago, more than half (59 percent) of the victims of fatal firearm assaults were males aged 15–34 years.

Across the hemisphere, the communities from which at-risk persons originate and in which the acts of gun-related criminality tend to be concentrated bear many similarities. Called "ghettos" in North America, *barrios marginales, villas miseria, barrios callampa, pueblos jóvenes* or *favelas* in Latin America (depending on the country) and "garrison communities" in the Caribbean, they tend to be urban, densely populated and underserved, with lower than national levels of most social indicators and standards of living. The term "garrison community", originally described the urban enclaves of violence such as Trench Town in Jamaica, which supported the competing political parties in the 1960s and 1970s. Now it refers to those communities where poverty and violence combine to produce a space of high levels of personal insecurity for community residents. Not only in Jamaica, but also in Guyana (Buxton) and Haiti (Cité Soleil) as well as in Trinidad and Tobago (Laventille), these communities are the foci of crime and violence. . . .

Gun Control

Since there is no domestic manufacturing of firearms in the English-speaking Caribbean, one obvious option would be to ban guns altogether. Effectiveness of such a measure is highly debatable, however, as shown by the experiences in other countries. In fact, opponents of gun control laws point out that Jamaica, despite banning guns, has had an increasing gun homicide rate, as did the United Kingdom and some states in Australia. Supporting this view is the fact that in various countries of the region, a "gun-for-rent" market has emerged, effectively sidestepping potential supply reductions. However, various measures can be put in place that can make gun control more effective.

Most gun control legislation in the Caribbean is aimed principally at legally acquired firearms, is poorly enforced, and has little impact on illicit guns. A systematic strategy that is more likely to be effective is one that first addresses the acquisition of illegal firearms, as it is believed that only a minority of registered arms are used to commit crimes. The first step in blocking the illicit trafficking of light arms would involve tight controls of vendor and purchaser, with strictly enforced regulations governing:

- Local sales with thorough background checks, close scrutiny of purchasers to deter the use of "straw purchasers" and an index of suspicious persons who purchase more than one gun in a stipulated time period. Annual inspection and licensing of firearms with follow-up may also serve as a deterrent.

- Exportation of firearms with documented approval after thorough checks by the supplying or manufacturing state on the *bona fides* of the purchasers, the use to which the firearms would be put and verification of their final destination. These checks should involve the authorities of the receiving state including the issuance of an import license.

- Importation of firearms with the issuance of an import license by the authorities of the purchaser's state.

- Transfer of firearms as *per* exportation and importation with notification of the supplier state.

- Preventing the illicit trafficking in light arms is a responsibility to be shared among the producing, selling, and destination states, whether intermediary or end users, with open and transparent communication among all. A good place to start is with the signing, ratification, and enforcement of international treaties and conventions such as the United Nations Protocol [Against] the Illicit [Manufacturing of and] Trafficking in Firearms[, Their Parts and Components and Ammunition] and the Organization of American States' Inter-American Convention Against Illicit Manufacturing of and Trafficking in Firearms, Ammunition, Explosives, and Other Related Materials [CIFTA]. Many states in the region have not signed, much less ratified, these international agreements.

"Preventing the illicit trafficking in light arms is a responsibility to be shared among the producing, selling, and destination states, whether intermediary or end users, with open and transparent communication among all."

Other Strategies for Regulation

Until cessation of the black market trade in light firearms becomes a reality, a "stop-gap" measure is to thwart as effectively as possible all efforts to land illegal guns. For the island countries of the Caribbean, this requires intensive surveillance of the coastline by naval police equipped with suitable watercraft. This is an expensive but necessary undertaking, especially for small island countries, as improved marine surveillance serves several purposes. Not only does it deter arms trafficking but also drug trafficking, piracy and trafficking in people.

The second means of illegal entry of firearms is their carriage through an official port of entry (air or sea) without detection. Legally entering yachtsmen or airline passengers, and their possessions, are subject to search by customs officers who are trained to seek dutiable goods and drugs, not firearms. To stem this, it is imperative that customs officers be trained to search for guns, to be able to recognize their component parts and to be aware of the methods of concealment of firearms and ammunition.

"These protocols need to apply to civilian users, rifle clubs, private security firms, police services, and the defense force."

The final source of firearms for use in criminal activity is the in-country diversion of legally acquired firearms and ammunition to illegal use. To prevent the reuse of weapons in gun-related crimes, it is critical that guns should be traceable and that weapons seized should be securely stored and properly disposed of. This requires effective procedures for acquisition, marking, licensing, registration, operation and storage. National gun registries are rare in the Caribbean. Licensing and use of firearms should also include an emphasis on the control of and accountability for ammunition, and not just for the firearm. Careful oversight needs to be given to the secure storage of firearms (both private and public storage), with clear guidelines on storage requirements, strict control with rigorous inspection procedures including a checklist, reporting format, periodicity, audits of ammunition and general accountability. These protocols need to apply to civilian users, rifle clubs, private security firms, police services, and the defense force.

Firearms enforcement requires police officers with the necessary forensic technology and knowledge to effectively gather, preserve and present evidence. This technology should include a forensic facility that especially provides for firearm forensics and ballistic examinations required for solving gun-related crimes. For every state to possess this facility may be burdensome and expensive. But it should certainly be possible to have it available in the largest Caribbean states or, at the very least, as a shared regional resource. The establishment of a "Gun Court", such as the one Jamaica has had since 1974, would expedite the processing of firearms cases.

Analysis of the situation with respect to gun-related criminality, the investigation and solving of cases, the monitoring of interventions, all require data—which does not currently exist in an easily accessible or useable form. Furthermore, with respect to guns and criminality, given the linkages with other countries within the Caribbean region and on the American and European continents, this data needs to be compatible and comparable so that it may be shared among all stakeholders. Registries with information on purchasers, gun markings and tracings, databases on ballistics, on gun transfers and movements are but a few of the useful data tools in the fight against guns and crime. Mechanisms need to be instituted for the sharing of information within countries across agencies and sectors and across countries to facilitate the tracking of firearms used in the commission of crimes and the identification of persons engaged in the smuggling of firearms.

Japan Is Active in the Global Arms Trade

Robin Ballantyne

Robin Ballantyne is a researcher at the Omega Research Foundation, an organization based in the United Kingdom, which studies the human rights impact of international transfers of military, security, and police (MSP) technologies. In the following viewpoint, she argues that despite its public claims of support for worldwide arms legislation, Japan is deeply involved in the global arms trade. Through the exporting of small firearms and by supplying international armies with weapons, she maintains, Japan is an intricate part of a business—both legal and illegal—that claims hundreds of thousands of lives each year.

As you read, consider the following questions:

1. As described by the author, how does the Japanese government define "arms"?

2. About how many people worldwide are killed by small arms each year?

3. According to the author, when did Japan begin to take advantage of the loophole in the ban on small arms exports?

The 2004 government announcement that it was considering joining the US [United States] in the production of a missile defence system was deeply troubling to Japanese and

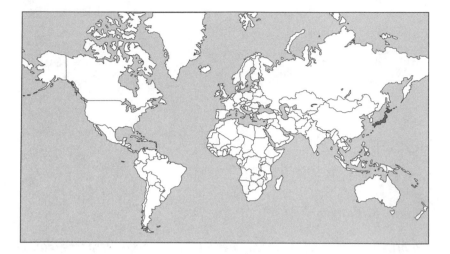

Asians concerned about Japan's expansive military posture in tandem with the US. Over the years, Japan has created a high-tech non-nuclear military force. But it has steadfastly maintained an official ban on weapons exports. Many feared that the move heralded the end of Japan's nearly 40-year-old ban on arms exports.

Since 1976, the Japanese government has proclaimed that "Japan shall not promote 'arms' exports, regardless of the destinations." This stance has been advanced by ministers and officials in the domestic and international arena, who stress that Japan does not participate in the global arms trade. For example, in 2000 Sugiura Seiken, the Senior Vice Minister for Foreign Affairs, informed a UN [United Nations] conference that: "Japan has been actively pursuing arms control and disarmament. We do not permit the export of arms to any country."

However, in December of 2004 it became clear that Japan's position as a weapons manufacturer and weapons exporter were under review. Not only was the Japanese government considering taking part in the Missile Defence Programme, but the Chief Cabinet Secretary also announced that Japan may consider other opportunities for joint development and production with the US, as well as projects with other countries "related to support of counterterrorism and counter-piracy." In addition, Prime Minister [Junichiro] Koizumi confirmed the possibility that Japan may sell arms to Southeast Asian nations to fight piracy.

"Far from having a record of no arms transfers, Japan has been and continues to be actively involved in the sale of small arms and dual-use goods to other nations."

These statements, and particularly the Missile Defence project, are being undertaken both in response to rising Japan-North Korea tensions, and in the wish to strengthen the capacity of Southeast Asian countries to protect Japanese shipping through the Malacca straits.

However, the truth of the matter is that these plans do not indicate a dramatic change in policy. Far from having a record of no arms transfers, Japan has been and continues to be actively involved in the sale of small arms and dual-use goods to other nations. Due to a lack of transparency in the reporting system, however, important questions remain concerning the precise nature of various military exports.

Small Arms

Japan has been one of the lead actors in the 2001 UN Programme of Action to Prevent, Combat and Eradicate the Illicit Trade in Small Arms and Light Weapons in All Its Aspects (PoA). It has donated substantial sums of money for various weapons collection programmes worldwide, most notably, over $10 million for programmes in Sri Lanka, Cambodia and Sierra Leone. Furthermore, Japan continues to campaign for the establishment of an international system to mark and trace small arms.

As the former Japanese ambassador to the Conference on Disarmament stated, Japan has assumed this lead role on the

PoA because " . . . many countries felt that Japan is the standard-bearer of multilateral disarmament affairs because Japan enjoys the high moral ground of not exporting small arms." However the fact is that Japan actually conducts a thriving small arms export trade. The international annual publication, the Small Arms Survey, for example, reported that in 2002 Japan exported $65 million worth of small arms which, in monetary terms, ranks Japan amongst the top eight exporters of small arms worldwide for that year.

The Japanese government evades this issue by contending that 'hunting guns and sport guns are not regarded as "arms"' and therefore the self-imposed ban on arms exports only applies to guns of a military specification. This raises the question of what differentiates a military specification gun from a sporting or hunting weapon. However, the Japanese Ministry [of Economy], Trade and Industry (METI) provides no comprehensive definition. Instead it decides on a case-by-case basis whether or not a weapon should be defined as being of military specification.

"When one is looking down the barrel of a gun it matters little whether the weapon in question is deemed to be of the sporting or hunting or military variety."

The finessing of the definition of "arms" to exclude sporting and hunting weapons may ensure that Japan adheres to its ban on arms in the eyes of the policy makers but in reality this is a cynical interpretation. While METI claims that there is a distinction between a sporting weapon and a military weapon, the fact of the matter is that almost all tactical shotguns—the type of weapon used by military and police forces throughout the world—are modified civilian guns.

Each year small arms kill approximately 500,000 people around the world. So great is their impact on human security that [former Secretary-General of the UN] Kofi Annan observed: "In terms of the carnage they cause, small arms, indeed, could well be described as 'weapons of mass destruction.'" The small arms used in these deaths are not restricted to those of a military specification. In armed conflicts around the world hunting and sporting weapons are routinely used to commit violent acts and abuse human rights. In recent years Amnesty International has reported the use of such weapons by death squads in Algeria and armed political groups in the Solomon Islands. Clearly, when one is looking down the barrel of a gun it matters little whether the weapon in question is deemed to be of the sporting or hunting or military variety.

Questionable Exports

Further questions about Japan's dedication to a ban on arms exports are raised by an examination of data submitted to the UN Commodity Trade Statistics database (Comtrade) which records the import and export details voluntarily submitted by the Customs departments of countries worldwide. According to information submitted by the Japanese Customs department to this database, in 2001 Japan exported US$55.7 million worth of "bombs, grenades, ammunition, mines, & others." The vast majority of this total went to the US. However, according to the import data submitted by other countries, other recipients of this equipment from Japan included Denmark, Germany, South Korea, Malaysia and Thailand.

Furthermore, according to information that Japan submitted to the Comtrade database in 1999, Japan exported "military weapons" to Indonesia and Malaysia and in 2000 Japan exported "military weapons" to Israel. Also according to the data submitted by Japan, it has exported "parts & accessories of military weapons" to a large number of countries over several years. And in 2003 Japan reported that it had exported "military rifles, machine guns and other" to the Philippines.

Japanese Customs uses the same system of classification for registering exports as does the UN. This means that the

Japan's Export Ban

Despite its 62-year-old constitution's proscriptions, Japan began conducting international arms sales in 1953. A ban on sales was first introduced under Prime Minister Satō Eisaku in 1967, though it only forbade trade with what were termed the '3 Ps'; states sponsoring terrorism, involved in conflict or under UN arms embargos. In 1976 it was expanded to include all countries though in 1983 Prime Minister Nakasone Yasuhiro granted the US a case-by-case exemption, the first major use of which was the decision in 2004 to allow joint research into Ballistic Missile Defense (BMD). This was followed in 2006 by a decision to permit the export of related technology to the United States. This was hailed as "a significant step forward" by Nippon Keidanren, the Japan Business Federation, and it pushed shares of Mitsubishi Heavy Industries up more than 35% in 2007. Concerns have been expressed by both the Keidanren and the Defence Ministry, that similar future ventures might not be possible should export restrictions remain.

Gavan Gray,
"Japan's Weapons Industry," GlobalResearch.ca, July 13, 2009.
www.globalresearch.ca.

Japanese definition of an export will be consistent with the UN definition. So when, for example, Japanese Customs reports that "military rifles, machine guns and other" have been exported, according to the UN definition that means that the export must have contained one of the following: self-propelled artillery weapons; rocket launchers; flamethrowers; grenade launchers; torpedo; torpedo tubes and similar or other. Of course a note of caution must be added in that the "other" at the end of the list may refer to a number of different items ranging from military rifles to optical devices for use on firearms. Although the Japanese Customs chooses to subdivide the categories when they submit information to Comtrade, thus providing a greater level of detail, even this information does not give a sufficiently detailed breakdown of exactly what items were in the export.

Since there is no domestic report of arms exports, and the information submitted to Comtrade is sufficiently vague as to prevent any meaningful analysis, it is impossible to verify the exact nature of the equipment in these transfers. Until the Japanese government reveals details of these exports, questions will remain as to whether they complied with the "no arms trade" policy.

Dual-Use Goods

A bright light is shone on Japan's involvement in the arms trade when one examines exports of defence electronics and dual-use equipment. Ever since its inception, a gaping hole has existed in the ban on arms exports; specifically, products that have both military and civilian applications may escape the ban on military exports. In the 1980s Japanese companies began taking advantage of this loophole by making inroads mainly into the US defence market, providing semiconductor chips for guided missiles and camera lenses used in reconnaissance systems. Since then Japanese components have found their way into a large number of security and defence products across the globe, such as silicon sensors, which are at the core of BAE Systems' inertial measurement units used for missile guidance systems, or the Sony Exwave-HAD 800 Line TV camera incorporated in the Denel military and paramilitary turrets.

It seems that even certain vehicles used by the military are able to evade the export ban by using the dual-use window of opportunity. Military forces throughout the world can be seen riding Toyotas, Suzukis and Mitsubishis. In March of this year

[2005] the Engine Engineering Company announced that it would be basing its Nimer-1 light armoured personnel carrier on a Toyota Land Cruiser 4x4 chassis. The vehicle, which will have firing ports and the possibility of mounted machine guns, is clearly for military use, yet because the Land Cruiser chassis can also be exported for civilian use, it escapes the ban on arms exports. In August 2004 ShinMaywa promoted its US-1A amphibious aircraft designed for search and rescue but also for maritime patrol and anti-submarine warfare roles. While the assistant manager of defence systems at the company acknowledged that Japan is prohibited from exporting defence systems, he insisted that the craft was available for purchase and could be used for "multipurpose missions."

"The essential problem when analyzing Japan's adherence to its 'no arms trade' policy is the lack of transparency."

Transparency and Truth

The essential problem when analysing Japan's adherence to its "no arms trade" policy is the lack of transparency in the reporting of the export licences that have been granted for goods used in the defence industry. Although Japan makes annual submissions to UN databases regarding its exports, these submissions are voluntary and, as can be seen from the Comtrade data above, do not always tally with what other countries claim to be receiving from Japan. More importantly, unlike many other countries such as Germany, Finland, UK [United Kindgom] or USA, the Japanese government provides no annual report detailing the licences that it has granted for arms or goods used in the defence industry. This means that the Japanese public and press have no access to information concerning what defence goods may have been exported and whether these exports comply with the spirit or the letter of a policy banning arms exports.

It is nevertheless clear from the number of small arms and dual-use goods openly exported, that Japan has, for a number of years, had a fairly active arms trade, despite its declaration to the contrary. Japan's claim that it has no arms trade leaves it open to the charge of duplicity and deceit.

With the Japanese government proposing major changes related to weapons production and exports, now would surely be a time to provide an open and honest account of the nation's actual involvement in the arms trade, and to establish a formal system of reporting that lays to rest doubts about the military content of exports. Such information would end the hypocrisy and denial that currently reigns.

Russia's Place in the Global Arms Trade Is Uncertain

Collin Koh and Ron Matthews

Collin Koh is a research analyst and Ron Matthews is the deputy director of the Institute of Defence and Strategic Studies at the S. Rajaratnam School of International Studies at Nanyang Techno- logical University in Singapore. In the following viewpoint, they argue that Russia's share of the global arms market is eroding. To make up for this deficit, Russia has expanded its market to include countries that the West finds politically disagreeable, which could prove to be damaging in the future.

As you read, consider the following questions:

1. Compared to other nations, how does Russia rank in global arms exports?
2. As of January 2008, what percentage of Russia's defense companies were on the brink of bankruptcy?
3. By what percentage did China limit its imports of Russian arms in 2006–2007?

The recent capture by Somali pirates of a Ukrainian ship laden with Russian armaments highlights yet again the global reach of Russian arms exports. These arms, allegedly destined for Sudan, represent a microcosm of Russia's recent

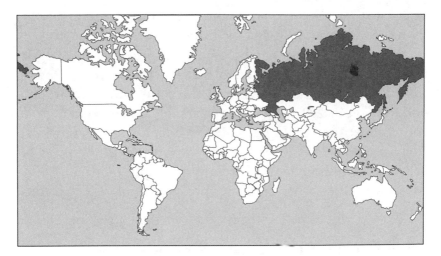

billion dollar deals to nations as far-flung as Indonesia and Venezuela. In the latter case, Russia raised the *ante* by also sending warships and long-range bombers to conduct joint military manoeuvres. Russia's expanded military and diplomatic influence, through the cultivation of arms sales, signals not only the rising competitiveness of Russian military kit but also perhaps the growth of global anti-US [United States] sentiment.

> *"But for substantial arms sales to China and India in the 1990s, Russia's military-industrial complex would not have survived."*

Choppy Waters Ahead?

Yet, but for substantial arms sales to China and India in the 1990s, Russia's military-industrial complex would not have survived. Vladimir Putin's succession as the president of Russia marked an end to the chaos then afflicting Russia's defence economy. Increased military appropriations afforded by huge energy revenues allowed new capital infusions into defence-related research and development. Also, a state decree which designated *Rosoboronexport* as the single arms trading authority helped reposition Russia in the global defence market.

Since then, Russia has become the world's second largest arms exporter after the United States, with earnings growth from US$3 billion at the close of the 20th century to around US$7 billion in 2007. This is a remarkable growth trend, given the competitive challenges Russia faces. However, whilst *Rosoboronexport*, as Russia's arms exporting agency, aims to sell US$6.1 billion worth of military equipment in 2008, Moscow's future arms exporting prospects look less than certain.

Russia's New Arms Export Reality

Russia's arms export successes since the late 1990s can be attributed mainly to sales of higher-end weapons. Having inherited substantial Cold War–era military hardware and industrial capacities within their territories, some of the former Soviet republics have become arms exporters in their own right, filling lower-end arms niches. Ukraine, for example, is ranked as the world's tenth largest arms supplier, marketing weapons equivalent to, yet cheaper than, Russian kit.

> *"These newer models thus challenge Russia's primacy in quality-price ratios, especially in the developing world's arms markets."*

Poland and Ukraine have also been actively promoting indigenous derivatives of the Soviet-era *T-72* main battle tank—33 of which are embroiled in the piracy of the Ukrainian vessel *MV Faina* and its Africa-bound lethal cargo. Yet, whilst the arms on the *MV Faina* are definitely of Russian design, mystery continues to surround the origins of this vessel's cargo and also its ultimate destination. Rumours have now surfaced that the shipment was handled by the Ukrainian arms exporter, *Ukrspetsexport*, and its destination was not Sudan, but another, as yet, unknown African country.

Due to the increased competition that Russia increasingly faces in the global arms market, *Rosoboronexport* has become obliged to market the more sophisticated hardware in its stable, including advanced *Sukhoi Su-27/30*-series fighters, submarines, *T-90* tanks and missile systems. Even in this high-end arena, Russia faces stiff competition from an emerging network of lower-order arms exporters. For instance, using original Russian technology, obtained through huge arms deals, China has been able to reverse-engineer hardware such as the *J-11* fighter—widely seen as a cheaper carbon copy of the high-tech *Su-27*–-with huge potential sales to the developing world's militaries.

Similarly, the new Chinese *PHL03* artillery rocket system bears striking resemblance to the Russian *9K58 'Smerch'*. While most Chinese makes are essentially duplicates of Cold War Soviet weapons, such as the *F-7* (*MiG-21*) fighter or the *Type-59/69* tank (*T-55*), emerging Chinese copies of high-end Russian hardware can increasingly compete with the 'originals' in terms of price competitiveness. These newer models thus challenge Russia's primacy in quality-price ratios, especially in the developing world's arms markets.

More Attractive Terms

To effectively compete in the international arms bazaar, Russia not only has to churn out newer and more sophisticated military technologies, but also has to offer more attractive terms, such as lower costs, and deal sweeteners, including credits and technology transfers. Sales of high-end equipment like *Su-30* fighters and *'Kilo'* class submarines have therefore created an export boom for Russia's defence contractors, positioning them amongst the top echelon of global arms suppliers. Yet, surprisingly, Russian defence contractors are presently under enormous financial pressure. Notwithstanding the availability of funding underpinning state defence procurement, Russia's

The Five Largest Suppliers of Major Conventional Weapons, 2004–2008

Supplier	Share of Global Arms Exports (%)	Main Recipients (share of supplier's transfers)
USA	31	South Korea (15%) Israel (13%) UAE (11%)
Russia	25	China (42%) India (21%) Algeria (8%)
Germany	10	Turkey (15%) Greece (13%) South Africa (12%)
France	8	UAE (32%) Singapore (13%) Greece (12%)
UK	4	USA (21%) India (14%) Chile (9%)

TAKEN FROM: SIPRI Arms Transfer Database, 2009.

generals have complained about slow delivery and low quality of supposedly sophisticated hardware.

Foreign complaints have also surfaced. For instance, in May 2008 Algeria pointedly rejected further deliveries of the *MiG-29* fighter—another high-end Russian export—because of its inferior build quality. These woes are caused by an aging military-industrial infrastructure, high overhead and raw material costs, and declining quality of manpower. In January this year [2008], a senior Russian military-industrial official stated that 25% of the countries' defence companies are on the brink of bankruptcy. Deterioration in product quality has begun to affect even the high-end hardware that Russia aggressively markets abroad. Previous restructuring, such as the 'strategic' amalgamation of aerospace and maritime firms into separate and consolidated unitary corporations, have failed to ease these problems; rather they have engendered opportunities for corruption and mismanagement of state funds.

As the Stockholm International Peace Research Institute (SIPRI) noted in March 2008, Russia's defence-industrial decay combined with Moscow's paranoia over potential technology leakage, is beginning to have an impact on established markets. China, for instance, has reduced imports of Russian arms by a gargantuan 62%, albeit over the limited period, 2006–2007. In the face of potentially shrinking import orders from traditional major markets and a threatened reduction in its share of the global arms trade, Russia has sought to peddle arms to new, and some times less demanding, clients.

Such sales may be at the expense of contravening international norms and clashing with Western interests. Despite having ruled out unauthorized arms exports to conflict areas, Moscow can be tempted. An example of this is the alleged sale of *MiG-29s*—allegedly through Belarus—to Sudan; this carried with it the further unwanted controversy surrounding the reported death of a Russian *MiG-29* pilot during last May's Darfur fighting.

"Notwithstanding its record-breaking sales over recent years, the prospects for Russia's arms exports are shrouded in uncertainty."

Emerging Dilemma for Russia's Arms Exports

Russia's arms export prospects will be shaped by an emerging dilemma. On the one hand, Russia aspires to become the world's top arms supplier, expanding its share of the market while retaining traditional large buyers such as China and India. On the other hand, in order to sell more arms in the highly competitive global defence market, Russia needs to push incentive deals, such as technology transfer, but with the caveat, of course, that such transfers may act to undermine national security.

To circumvent this, and to cope with the real, or potential, threat of new-entry high-end arms sellers offering competitive contractual packages, Russia will be obliged to expand the geographical scope of its arms sales, as evident in Russia's recent forays into Southeast Asia and Latin America. Yet, Moscow's arms trade with such countries, especially those shunned by Western states, will likely be mired in controversy. Notwithstanding its record-breaking sales over recent years, the prospects for Russia's arms exports are shrouded in uncertainty.

Costa Rica's Small Arms Regulations Should Be Adopted Internationally

Oscar Arias Sánchez

In the following viewpoint, Oscar Arias Sánchez, the president of Costa Rica, argues that other world countries would benefit socially, economically, and in many other ways if they implemented Costa Rica's policies on firearms. In addition to banning the sale of guns, Costa Rica no longer has a military. Instead, monies that were once used for arms and soldiers are now used for education and social programs. In turn, Costa Rica and its people have thrived. The only way the world will progress, asserts Sánchez, is by investing more time and money in social betterment than in wars and weaponry.

As you read, consider the following questions:

1. Annually how much money does the world spend on arms and soldiers?

2. As explained by Sánchez, what was promised in Monterrey, Mexico, in 2002?

3. As explained by Sánchez, what is the main message of the International Code of Conduct on Arms Transfers?

Oscar Arias Sánchez, "The Global Arms Trade: Strengthening International Regulations: An Interview with Oscar Arias Sánchez," *Harvard International Review*, vol. 30, summer, 2008, pp. 1–8. Copyright © 2008 *The Harvard International Review*. Reproduced by permission.

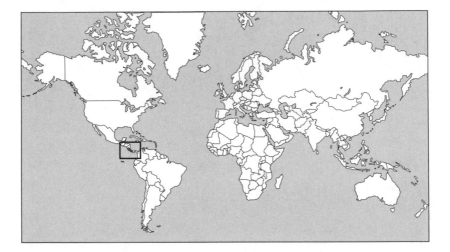

Climate Change: Mr. President, you are internationally recognized as an advocate on behalf of the developing world. How has the international arms trade—"licit" and illicit— affected the economic growth of the world's poorest nations? More specifically, how has weapons trading impacted the economies of Latin America?

Oscar Arias Sánchez: For more than 20 years, I have made peace and demilitarization a personal mission. Today, as President of Costa Rica for a second term, I have challenged the international community to redefine its priorities. When a country decides to invest in arms, rather than in education, housing, the environment, and health services for its people, it is depriving a whole generation of its right to prosperity and happiness.

Global expenditure on arms and soldiers is more than one trillion dollars per year. That's approximately US$3.3 billion per day. This staggering misallocation of resources is a brutal demonstration of the skewed priorities and values in many societies. We have produced one firearm for every ten inhabitants of this planet, and yet we have not bothered to end hunger when such a feat is well within our reach. By a conservative estimate, we turn out eight million small arms per year, and yet we have not managed to ensure that all our children receive a decent education. This is not a necessary or inevitable state of affairs. It is a deliberate choice.

The consequences of that choice for the developing world are devastating. The governments of some of the poorest nations on Earth, including some from Latin America, continue to squander millions on troops, tanks and missiles. In 2006, the region's military spending was over US$32 billion, while 194 million people languished in poverty. Latin America has begun a new arms race, regardless of the fact that the region has never been more democratic; regardless of the fact that in the last century it has rarely seen military conflicts between nations; regardless of the fact that a host of dire needs in the fields of education and public health demand attention. We understand now more than ever that the educational catastrophes of today are the economic catastrophes of tomorrow, and yet some leaders continue to make war their priority, instead of children.

"When a country decides to invest in arms . . . it is depriving a whole generation of its right to prosperity and happiness."

Ironically, this mistake leaves Latin America less safe than before—because investment in education is not just an investment in the future prosperity of our economies. It is also a consolidation of democracy, and a safeguard against a return to the authoritarian political culture that has marred and bloodied our history. Failing to make this investment weakens our resistance to those authoritarian temptations, weakens our defense against the demagoguery of some populists, and weakens us against the extremist ideology that lies beneath some political organizations. Some governments justify their absurd military spending in the name of protecting their people, but by neglecting education and other social services, they risk the very democracy and liberty that our region has worked so hard to achieve.

Spending more on education and technology would involve sacrifices, of course. It would involve sacrifices like the money invested in every Sukhoi Su-30K aircraft, which costs approximately US$34 million; those funds could buy 200,000 MIT Media Lab computers for schools. It would involve sacrifices like the money invested in every Black Hawk helicopter, which costs approximately US$6 million; those funds could pay a US$100 monthly educational grant for 5,000 students for an entire year. The choice is clear.

Could you describe the goals of the Costa Rica Consensus? How does it aim to establish criteria for debt relief so as to reward nations that reduce arms spending?

As we all know, war is an industry, providing multimillion-dollar profits for companies and countries that engage in it. Peace threatens those profits, and often results in decreased support for those who achieve it. One needs to look no further than Central America for an eloquent example. Our peace process in the 1980s resulted in the withdrawal of foreign aid for a region that desperately needed resources to rebuild its countries and provide for its people.

In 1987, when the presidents of Central America signed the Esquipulas accords that ended the civil wars in our region, we asked for help. We wrote, "There are Central American ways to achieve peace and development, but we need assistance to make them a reality. [We ask for] international treatment that would guarantee [our] development so the peace we seek will be a lasting one."

When we took this step toward peace, we thought that help would come. But nations that sent money and arms with lightning speed during our time of war and darkness proved slow to shine their generosity upon us afterward. Though Central America has received small increases in development aid, the total is still far less than the aid wealthy countries sent when weapons and troops were involved. After 20 years, we all see a stark bottom line: Central America has been punished for achieving peace.

Some use the excuse that we are middle-income countries. They have told almost a million Costa Ricans who live in poverty that the rest of their country is too rich. They will tell countless Central Americans who go to bed hungry that their per capita GDP [gross domestic product] is rising too fast. They will continue to tell 40 percent of the world's poor, the millions and millions who live in middle-income countries, that other people within their national borders are too well-off for them to deserve help. Central America's poor were once victims of political ideologies. Now they are victims of a statistical average.

"We Costa Ricans want to see more of our brothers and sisters in the developing world enjoy the same dividends."

Then came Monterrey. In 2002, world leaders met in Monterrey, Mexico, and made a bold promise: Developed nations would dedicate 0.7 percent of their GDP to development aid. The fight against AIDS, the conservation of our environment, and the education of our young people would finally get the resources they deserve. Even if countries were classified as "middle-income," there would be enough aid to reach them. In Central America, we thought, "Now help will come." But very little has arrived. Monterrey was a promissory note that almost no one has decided to honor.

A framework to change this destructive pattern and to use foreign aid as an incentive, rather than a deterrent, to reduce military spending is long overdue. Just as Central America is a perfect example of the need for such a change, Costa Rica is a natural leader for this effort. We may be one of the smallest countries on Earth, but our commitment to peace is great. In

1948, President José Figueres took a visionary step when he abolished our country's military and declared peace on the world. This decision set Costa Rica apart from the rest of Latin America, and paid off in strong education and health care systems, a highly educated workforce, political stability, and modern infrastructure. Today, Costa Rica seeks to become a developed country by year 2021, when we celebrate 200 years of independence.

We have reaped the benefits of peace—but that is not enough. We Costa Ricans want to see more of our brothers and sisters in the developing world enjoy the same dividends. We want to see other leaders encouraged to make the brave and productive choice that our President Figueres once made. Therefore, in 2006, my administration presented before the United Nations the Costa Rica Consensus, which establishes new criteria for extending credit to developing nations and forgiving their debt. It asks wealthy nations to consider not only a country's income, but also how it spends that money.

For how can the wounds of sub-Saharan Africa be healed if the region's governments are provided money that they then use to buy more grenades, helicopters, and AK-47s, perpetuating the poverty of their people? How can the poorest countries in Latin America move forward if existing aid structures encourage their leaders to arm themselves against a nonexistent enemy? It is time that we create mechanisms to forgive the debt of developing nations that invest more in education, health, and environmental protection, and less in soldiers and weapons. It is time that the international financial community reward those who use resources morally, rather than turning a blind eye to preventable suffering,

That is the Costa Rica Consensus. I hope the international community will give it life.

In what ways is the current body of international agreements failing to regulate the arms trade? What regional and global

Upper-Middle-Income Economies

Algeria	Grenada	Peru
American Samoa	Jamaica	Poland
Argentina	Kazakhstan	Romania
Belarus	Latvia	Russian Federation
Bosnia and Herzegovina	Lebanon	Serbia
Botswana	Libya	Seychelles
Brazil	Lithuania	South Africa
Bulgaria	Macedonia, FYR	St. Kitts and Nevis
Chile	Malaysia	St. Lucia
Colombia	Mauritius	St. Vincent and the Grenadines
Costa Rica	Mayotte	Suriname
Cuba	Mexico	Turkey
Dominica	Montenegro	Uruguay
Dominican Republic	Namibia	Venezuela, RB
Fiji	Palau	
Gabon	Panama	

World Bank Group,
"Country Classification," July 2009.
www.web.worldbank.org.

regulations are currently in place and how are they inadequate in addressing the problem of arms trade?

Where can I begin? Our international regulations allow almost three-quarters of all global arms sales to pour into the developing world with no binding international guidelines whatsoever. Our regulations do not hold countries accountable for what is done with the weapons they sell, even when the probable use of such weapons is obvious. Our regulations do not apply to arms transfers to individuals, even when the risk for wanton destruction is just as severe as in a transaction between states. Our regulations do not cover all conventional weapons, even though helicopter gunships and armed Humvees can be just as deadly as pistols and rifles.

Many of the existing regional, sub-regional, and multilateral arrangements lack clear definitions of the arms to which they apply; they lack a framework for enforcement, monitoring, and verification; and most importantly, they lack consistent political will by signatory states. The 2001 United Nations Programme of Action to Prevent, Combat, and Eradicate the Illicit Trade in Small Arms and Light Weapons in All Its Aspects [PoA] has proven to be less effective than originally intended, precisely due to its voluntary nature and failure to mention specific ammunition.

For years, you and fellow Nobel Laureates have advocated a formal, international Arms Trade Treaty (ATT). How would the ATT improve upon and/or formalize existing agreements?

In 1997, I met with seven other Nobel Peace Laureates in New York City to draft an International Code of Conduct on Arms Transfers. Our idea was simple—so simple, in fact, that it is hard to believe it is not yet a part of international law. The Code of Conduct stated that countries must not transfer weapons if there is reason to believe the weapons will be used to violate human rights.

The Code also laid out other provisions to that end. It called for all international transfers of arms to be authorized by a recognized state and executed in agreement with national laws and procedures that reflect, as minimal criteria, the obligations of the states according to international law. It called for all countries to present annual national reports on the arms transfer before an international registry. It called for common norms that apply to all conventional weapons, transfers to individuals and other non-state actors, brokering, shipment, and dual use.

The Arms Trade Treaty [ATT] grew out of this Code of Conduct, is based on these same principles, and has gathered immense support from countries around the world.

In order to be effective, the ATT must be both universal and binding. What measures must be taken to achieve this result? What will be the United Nations' role in enforcing the treaty and what responsibilities will fall on individual governments?

First and foremost, there must be real political will on behalf of all member states in the implementation of an Arms Trade Treaty. Genuine progress toward better controls on arms commerce will remain stagnant if changes are not enacted at all levels: national, regional, and global. Therefore, in order for an ATT to be truly effective, it is imperative that it be universal, legally binding, and include all conventional arms, together with small arms and light weapons (SALW) and ammunition.

"Genuine progress toward better controls on arms commerce will remain stagnant if changes are not enacted on all levels."

Nearly all acts of modern warfare, terrorism, organized crime, and gang violence are primarily perpetrated with SALW. The abundance and relative ease of acquisition of these weapons in regions of conflict has only served to exacerbate existing conditions of poverty, social violence, and insecurity, ultimately hindering development and citizen well-being. The need to include small arms and ammunition in the treaty is undeniable; it is our global responsibility to do so. Amidst the complex, technical aspects the treaty will naturally contain, we must remember our moral imperative to stop the flow of weapons that are used to violate human rights.

Designing an appropriate system of monitoring is certainly one of the foremost challenges facing those who bring the treaty to life. To ensure transparency and compliance, we must establish a system of information sharing. The United Nations could serve as a neutral entity in charge of the management and distribution of information. Individual governments will provide the data, and indeed, much of the success of the treaty will depend on the honest, reliable implementation carried out at the national level. The ATT will require individual governments to create or strengthen their own laws and policies in this area as needed; the treaty, in turn, will provide a standard set of rules to facilitate transparent and verifiable arms transactions between countries.

In 2006, the Small Arms Review Conference held in New York City ended without agreement. What have been the major obstacles to the successful passage of the ATT? Do you envision progress and cooperation among states in the future on this issue?

The lack of advancement with the PoA initiative is one of many reasons why, now more than ever, I believe it is time for a comprehensive Arms Trade Treaty. Although there is a long road ahead for the treaty, significant progress has been made.

"It is time for us to right this terrible wrong."

In 2006, the United Nations General Assembly approved a resolution ordering the Secretary-General to create a Group of Governmental Experts to examine the feasibility, scope and draft parameters of an eventual Arms Trade Treaty. Throughout this year, members of this group are meeting periodically. I am confident that this group will reach a consensus regarding the urgency of an ATT.

Undoubtedly, we face differences of opinion. Some delegations disagree about whether the treaty should cover all conventional weapons, which, as I have mentioned, is essential. Others argue that the proposed guidelines infringe on a nation's right to defend its security interests. But there is no security in arms. There is not a single shred of evidence suggesting that the arms race has created a safer world. On the contrary, the arms trade and the proliferation of small guns in the hands of our children and citizens have made us more vulnerable as a species, and have made us poorer. As long as there are 875 million firearms in the world and the number increases every day, any peace is just a brief and fragile truce. What's more, I think we can all agree that no legitimate security interest is ever served by providing weapons to those who seek to violate human rights.

President Dwight D. Eisenhower once said that "every gun that is made, every warship launched, every rocket fired, signifies in the final sense a theft from those who hunger and are not fed, those who are cold and are not clothed." This world is not only squandering its resources; it is squandering the sweat of its workers, the genius of its scientists and the hope of its children. We have stayed on that destructive and reckless path for decades. It is time for us to right this terrible wrong.

Periodical Bibliography

The following articles have been selected to supplement the diverse views presented in this chapter.

David A. Andelman   "Onward to Armageddon?" *World Policy Journal*, vol. 26, no. 3, Fall 2009.

Jana Arsovska and Panos A. Kostakos   "Illicit Arms Trafficking and the Limits of Rational Choice Theory: The Case of the Balkans," *Trends in Organized Crime*, December 2008.

Mark Bromley   "The Europeanisation of Arms Export Policy in the Czech Republic, Slovakia, and Poland," *European Security*, vol. 16, no. 2, 2007.

Paul Cornish   "Gun Control," *World Today*, October 1, 2008.

Guy Lamb and Dominique Dye   "African Solutions to an International Problem: Arms Control and Disarmament in Africa," *Journal of International Affairs*, Spring/Summer 2009.

Rhona MacDonald   "Where Next for Arms Control," *Lancet*, vol. 368, no. 9537, August 26, 2006.

Kennedy Agade Mkutu   "Disarmament in Karamoja, Northern Uganda: Is This a Solution for Localised Violent Inter- and Intra-Communal Conflict?" *Round Table: The Commonwealth Journal of International Affairs*, February 2008.

Kennedy Agade Mkutu   "Small Arms and Light Weapons Among Pastoral Groups in the Kenya-Uganda Border Area," *African Affairs*, vol. 106, no. 422, January 2007.

Rebecca Peters   "Small Arms: No Single Solution," *UN Chronicle*, vol. 46, no. 1–2, 2009.

Rachel Stohl and Doug Tuttle   "The Small Arms Trade in Latin America," *NACLA Report on the Americas*, March/April 2008.

For Further Discussion

Chapter 1

1. Of the global gun control polices discussed in this chapter, which one do you find most effective? Least effective? Explain your answers.

Chapter 2

1. Kevin Yuill argues that taking guns away from citizens will not save lives. Do you agree or disagree with his argument? Explain your answer.

2. After considering the arguments made by the Coalition for Gun Control and Simon Chapman and his colleagues, do you agree that stricter gun laws reduce violent crimes such as domestic violence? Why or why not?

Chapter 3

1. Thomas Jackson argues that stopping the proliferation of small arms across the globe is a challenge that must be tackled by government and nongovernmental agencies. However, both Human Rights Watch and David B. Kopel, Paul Gallant, and Joanne D. Eisen assert that gun confiscation programs conducted by the United Nations have led to human rights abuses. Using the viewpoints in this chapter, discuss better ways in which small arms can be collected.

2. Arthur Williams argues that gun control reforms in Jamaica are necessary to protect the well-being of children and adolescents. Based on the evidence he provides, do you agree with him? Or do you agree with Michael Farris who asserts that stricter gun control laws violate the rights of world citizens and do not protect children?

Chapter 4

1. Integrated Regional Information Networks (IRIN) calls for stricter regulation of the international small arms trade, and Collin Koh and Ron Matthews argue that Russia must do the same. Do you think passage of a global arms trade treaty is the answer, as Brian Wood argues? Why or why not?

2. Oscar Arias Sánchez, the president of Costa Rica, argues that other world countries would benefit if they implemented Costa Rica's firearms policies, which include bans on the sale of guns and the abolishment of a military force. Do you think his radical plan would be effective for the rest of the world? Why or why not?

Organizations to Contact

The editors have compiled the following list of organizations concerned with the issues debated in this book. The descriptions are derived from materials provided by the organizations. All have publications or information available for interested readers. The list was compiled on the date of publication of the present volume—the information provided here may change. Be aware that many organizations take several weeks or longer to respond to inquiries, so allow as much time as possible.

Amnesty International (AI)

5 Penn Plaza, 16th Floor, New York, NY 10001
(212) 807-8400 • fax: (212) 463-9193
e-mail: admin-us@aiusa.org
Web site: www.amnesty.org

Amnesty International (AI) is a worldwide movement of people who campaign for internationally recognized human rights. By providing articles, publications, pamphlets, and video media, AI seeks to educate people about all human rights violations and call people to action. AI prints regular reports about gun control and small arms proliferation, including "Afghanistan: Abduction and Rape at the Point of a Gun" and "Almost One in Three People Affected by Gun Crime."

Coalition for Gun Control (CGC)

PO Box 90062, 1488 Queen Street W
Toronto, Ontario M6K 3K3
  Canada
(416) 604-0209
e-mail: 71417.763@compuserve.com
Web site: www.guncontrol.ca

Founded in the wake of a massacre in Montreal, Canada, the Coalition for Gun Control (CGC) works to reduce gun death, injury, and crime. The CGC supports legislation that argues for possession permits that are periodically renewed for all gun owners, a cost-effective system to register all guns, a total ban on assault weapons and large-capacity magazines, controls on the sale of ammunition, and tougher restrictions on handguns. In addition to fact sheets and commentaries, the CGC publishes reports about guns and gun crimes in Canada, including "Border Controls in Canada: Impact on Illicit Trafficking and Public Safety."

Disarmament and Security Centre (DSC)

PO Box 8390, Christchurch, Aotearoa
 New Zealand
64 3-348-1353
Web site: www.disarmsecure.org

In 1998, the Disarmament and Security Centre (DSC) was established as a specialist center of the Peace Foundation. The broad objective of the DSC is to provide a resource center for alternative thinking on disarmament and security issues, both within Aotearoa, New Zealand, and internationally. In addition to links to books written by the organization, the DSC Web site provides full-text articles, including "Pacific Connections: Women and the Peace Movement in Aotearoa."

International Action Network on Small Arms (IANSA)

Development House, 56-64 Leonard Street
London   EC2A 4LT
 United Kingdom
44-207-065-0870 • fax: 44-207-065-0871
e-mail: contact@iansa.org
Web site: www.iansa.org

The International Action Network on Small Arms (IANSA) is the global movement against gun violence. The IANSA is a network of eight hundred civil society organizations working in 120 countries to stop the proliferation and misuse of small arms and light weapons (SALW). In addition to fact sheets, such as "Gun Violence, a Global Academic," IANSA regularly publishes research reports about global gun issues, including *Reviewing Action on Small Arms 2006: Assessing the First Five Years of the Programme of Action.*

Jews for the Preservation of Firearms Ownership (JPFO)
PO Box 270143, Hartford, WI   53027
(262) 673-9745 • fax: (262) 673-9746
e-mail: jpfo@jpfo.org
Web site: www.jpfo.org

The goal of Jews for the Preservation of Firearms Ownership (JPFO) is to destroy gun control initiatives and to encourage Americans to understand and defend the Bill of Rights, especially the Second Amendment right to bear arms. Initially aimed at educating the Jewish community about the historical evils that Jews have suffered when they have been disarmed, JPFO has always welcomed persons of all religious beliefs who share a common goal of opposing and reversing victim disarmament policies while advancing liberty for all. In addition to links to their major publications, such as *Death by "Gun Control,"* JPFO's Web site provides access to numerous articles and other resources for fighting the adoption of gun control policies.

National Rifle Association of America (NRA)
11250 Waples Mill Road, Fairfax, VA   22030
(800) 672-3888
Web site: www.nra.org

While widely recognized today as a major political force and as America's foremost defender of Second Amendment rights, the National Rifle Association (NRA) has, since its inception in 1871, been the premier firearms education organization in the world. In 1990 the NRA established the tax-exempt NRA Foundation, which provides a means to raise millions of dollars to fund gun safety and educational projects of benefit to the general public. In addition to publishing a number of journals, such as *American Rifleman*, the NRA Web site features articles and columns written by members and organization officials.

Norwegian Initiative on Small Arms Transfers (NISAT)

c/o Preben Marcussen, Norwegian Red Cross
Hausmannsgate 7, Oslo   N-0133
  Norway
+47 22 05 41 66 • fax: +47 22 05 40 40
Web site: www.prio.no/NISAT/

The Norwegian Initiative on Small Arms Transfers (NISAT) was formed in December 1997 and is a coalition of the International Peace Research Institute (PRIO), Oslo, the Norwegian Red Cross, and Norwegian Church Aid. Its ultimate aim is to contribute to preventing and reducing armed violence. NISAT's Web site includes a large database on small arms transfers and a document library, which includes publications such as "Dangerous Dealings: Arms Brokering and Regulations in Southern Africa" and "Disarm or Perish: Is Disarmament a Necessary Condition for Peace?"

Regional Centre on Small Arms and Light Weapons (RECSA)

7th Floor, Timau Plaza, Arwings Khodek Road
PO Box 7039-00200, Nairobi
  Kenya
+254-20-3877456 • fax: +254-20-3877397
e-mail: info@recsasec.org
Web site: www.recsasec.org

The Regional Centre on Small Arms and Light Weapons (RECSA) is an institutional framework arising from the Nairobi Declaration of 2000 to coordinate the joint effort by National Focal Points in member states to prevent, combat, and eradicate stockpiling and illicit trafficking in small arms and light weapons in the Great Lakes region and the Horn of Africa. In addition, RECSA seeks to build the capacity of police and law enforcement officers to combat small arms proliferation and to develop partnerships between governments, civil society, and donor agencies to combat small arms proliferation. In addition to fact sheets, RECSA's Web site provides access to a number of the organization's publications, including the *RECSA Quarterly Bulletin* and RECSA's annual reports.

South Eastern and Eastern Europe Clearinghouse for the Control of Small Arms and Light Weapons (SEESAC)

Hadzi Milentijeva 30, Belgrade   11000
  Serbia
+381 11 344 6353 • fax: +380 11 344 6356
Web site: www.seesac.org

South Eastern and Eastern Europe Clearinghouse for the Control of Small Arms and Light Weapons (SEESAC) has a mandate from the United Nations Development Programme (UNDP) and the Regional Cooperation Council (RCC) to further support all international and national stakeholders by strengthening national and regional capacity to control and reduce the proliferation and misuse of small arms and light weapons. SEESAC's main goal is to enhance the stability, security, and development in Europe by reducing access to small arms. The SEESAC Web site provides access to many reports and other publications, including *Studies on Armed Violence* and *Reports on Trafficking.*

United Nations Office for Disarmament Affairs (UNODA)

Information and Outreach Branch, 220 East 42nd Street
Suite DN-2510, New York, NY   10017
fax: (212) 963-8995
e-mail: UNODA-web@un.org
Web site: www.un.org/disarmament

The United Nations Office for Disarmament Affairs (UNODA) was established in January 1998 and promotes the goal of nuclear disarmament and non-proliferation and the strengthening of the disarmament regimes in respect to other weapons of mass destruction and chemical and biological weapons. It also promotes disarmament efforts in the area of conventional weapons, especially land mines and small arms, which are the weapons of choice in contemporary conflicts. UNODA maintains an enormous database of research on arms and their proliferation across the world, including "Conflict of Interests: Children and Guns in Zones of Instability" and "Disarmament in Conflict Prevention."

Bibliography of Books

The following books have been selected to supplement the diverse views presented in this book.

Christopher Carr — *Kalashnikov Culture: Small Arms Proliferation and Irregular Warfare.* Westport, CT: Praeger Security International, 2008.

Holly Cefrey — *Gun Violence.* New York: Rosen Publishers, 2009.

Wendy Cukier and Victor W. Sidel — *The Global Gun Epidemic: From Saturday Night Specials to AK-47s.* Westport, CT: Praeger Security International, 2006.

Graduate Institute of International and Development Studies, Geneva, Switzerland — *Small Arms Survey 2008: Risk and Resilience.* Cambridge, UK: Cambridge University Press, 2008.

Bernard E. Harcourt — *Language of the Gun: Youth, Crime, and Public Policy.* Chicago: University of Chicago Press, 2006.

Rob Hornsby and Dick Hobbs, eds. — *Gun Crime.* Hants, England: Ashgate, 2008.

International Action Network on Small Arms — *The Impact of Guns on Women's Lives.* Oxford, England: Oxfam International, 2005.

Elli Kytömäki and Valerie Yankey-Wayne	*Five Years of Implementing the United Nations Programme of Action on Small Arms and Light Weapons: Regional Analysis of National Reports.* Geneva, Switzerland: United Nations Institute for Disarmament Research, 2006.
Emily B. Landau	*Arms Control in the Middle East: Cooperative Security Dialogue and Regional Constraints.* Brighton, England: Sussex Academic Press, 2006.
Wayne LaPierre	*The Global War on Your Guns: Inside the U.N. Plan to Destroy the Bill of Rights.* Nashville, TN: Nelson Current, 2006
Salma Malik and Mallika Joseph	*Small Arms and the Security Debate in South Asia.* New Delhi: Manohar Publishers and Distributors, 2005.
Jean L. Manore and Dale G. Miner, eds.	*The Culture of Hunting in Canada.* Vancouver, British Columbia, Canada: UBC Press, 2007.
Kennedy Agade Mkutu	*Guns and Governance in the Rift Valley: Pastoralist Conflict & Small Arms.* Oxford, UK: James Currey, 2008.
Howard Nemerov	*Four Hundred Years of Gun Control: Why Isn't It Working?* Lakewood, CA: Contrast Media Press, 2008.
Waheguru Pal Singh Sidhu and Ramesh Thakur, eds.	*Arms Control After Iraq: Normative and Operational Challenges.* Tokyo, Japan: United Nations University, 2006.

Katri K. Sieberg   *Criminal Dilemmas: Understanding and Preventing Crime.* Berlin: Springer, 2005.

Robert J. Spitzer   *The Politics of Gun Control.* Washington, DC: CQ Press, 2008.

Charles Fruehling Springwood, ed.   *Open Fire: Understanding Global Gun Cultures.* Oxford, UK: Berg, 2007.

Rachel Stohl, Matt Schroeder, and Dan Smith   *The Small Arms Trade: A Beginner's Guide.* Oxford, UK: Oneworld, 2007.

Taya Weiss   *Perpetrating Power: Small Arms in Post-Conflict Sierra Leone and Liberia.* Pretoria, South Africa: Institute for Security Studies, 2005.

Harry L. Wilson   *Guns, Gun Control, and Elections: The Politics and Policy of Firearms.* Lanham, MD: Rowman & Littlefield, 2007.

Index

Geographic headings and page numbers in **boldface** refer to viewpoints about that country or region.